GOING
TO
SALT LAKE CITY
TO DO
FAMILY
HISTORY
RESEARCH

GOING TO SALT LAKE CITY TO DO FAMILY HISTORY RESEARCH

J. Carlyle Parker

Second Edition, Revised and Expanded

Marietta Publishing Company
Turlock, California
1993

First Edition published 1989. Second Edition, Revised and Expanded 1993

Printed in the United States of America on acid free paper

Library of Congress Cataloging-in-Publication Data

Parker, J. Carlyle.
   Going to Salt Lake City to do family history research / by J. Carlyle Parker.
     p. cm.
   Includes bibliographical references.
   ISBN 0-934153-10-8 : $12.95
   1. Church of Jesus Christ of Latter-day Saints. Family History Library--Handbooks, manuals, etc. 2. Genealogical libraries--Utah--Salt Lake City--Handbooks, manuals, etc. 3. Genealogy--Library resources--Handbooks, manuals, etc. 4. Genealogy. I. Title.
Z733.C55P37 1993
026'.9291'0720792'258--dc20   92-29080
                                        CIP

OCLC #26398866

Ancestral File, *Family History Library Catalog*, *Family Registry*, *FamilySearch*, and *International Genealogical Index* are trademarks of the Corporation of the President of the Church of Jesus Christ of Latter-day Saints. *Personal Ancestral File* is a registered trademark of the Corporation of the President of the Church of Jesus Christ of Latter-day Saints. Some material in this publication is reprinted by permission of the Church of Jesus Christ of Latter-day Saints. In granting permission for this use of copyright materials, the Church does not imply or express either endorsement or authorization of this publication.

$12.95, plus $1.50 for shipping if ordered direct from publisher. Californians need to add sales tax at the percentage rate of their county of residence.

Marietta Publishing Company, 2115 North Denair Avenue, Turlock, CA 95380, (209) 634-9473, SAN 693-2002

To

Janet

CONTENTS

ILLUSTRATIONS

FLOOR PLANS

MAPS

PREFACE

The Family History Library continues to be the world's largest genealogical library. Since 1989, when *Going to Salt Lake City to Do Family History Research* was published, the Library's reported holdings have increased. The collection now consists of

> over 1.8 million reels (the equivalent of about 6 million volumes),
> approximately 325,000 microfiches (the equivalent of about 81,000 volumes),
> over 235,000 volumes of books.

The total equivalent is about 6,316,000 volumes.

The Library will continue to grow at a rapid rate. It currently adds about 100,000 reels (the equivalent of about 350,000 volumes) of microfilm per year, about 62,000 microfiche (the equivalent of about 13,000 volumes) per year, and about 10,000 volumes of books per year, for a total equivalent of about 373,000 volumes per year. At this growth rate the Library will add the equivalent of over one million volumes every three years. The Library is open to the public free of charge, except for a few small service fees that will be mentioned within this book.

This work contains much material about Family History Centers. They serve as satellite research centers to the Family History Library. There are about 1,650 Family History Centers which offer services such as interlibrary loan of microforms, photocopy requests, and reference questionnaire requests. Because use of these centers is free except for small service charges for borrowing, photocopying, or computer printouts, there is much research that you can accomplish without even going to Salt Lake City. This book will help you know what that research is. Books and certain microforms in the Library in Salt Lake City cannot be borrowed. But even these are not entirely outside your reach. Through your local public library you may borrow these materials from other libraries, as they may exist elsewhere, or you may hire independent researchers to search these materials for you.

Preface

It is easier to research in Salt Lake City than in Denmark, England, the Netherlands, and Sweden because in those countries the research sources are not collected in one centralized national archive.

In the interest of obtaining suggestions for improvement of this book, inquiries were made of seventy-eight purchasers of the first edition in the United States and Canada. A special thanks to them for their suggestions, many of which have been incorporated in the second edition.

Since the first edition of this work I have had the privilege of opening another Family History Center, in Turlock, California. I now serve as its volunteer director and am no longer the librarian and director of the Modesto California Family History Center, where I served for twenty-one years.

I am grateful to librarians and researchers who responded to my inquiries concerning published and unpublished state-wide indexes of biographical sketches, included in chapter 8. For this I owe thanks to the librarians of the Tutwiler Collection of Southern History, Birmingham Public Library, Birmingham, Alabama; David A. Hales, University of Alaska Fairbanks; Maine Historical Society; Dr. Roderick Thomas of Bar Harbor, Maine; and Carla Rickerson, University of Washington, in addition to those named in the Preface on pages xvi-xvii.

I am also grateful to the staff of the Family History Library who have assisted me as I have used the Library, and to A. Gregory Brown who provided most of the Library's photographs and floor plans. Sometime ago Kory L. Meyerink, Publications Coordinator of the Family History Library, invited me to permit him to review my works before publication. He has reviewed this work; and I am grateful to him for his suggestions, many of which have been implemented. Robert Davis and Ron Reed of the Museum of Church History and Art were very helpful in locating and permitting the use of the "Census Taker" photograph reprinted on page 54.

I couldn't have completed this work without the advice, suggestions, and proofreading assistance provided by Janet, my very supportive wife, and my son, Bret, another professional librarian in the family. The third librarian in the family, my daughter, Denise, and her husband, Paul Paxton, helped me with some recent updates concerning Family History Library changes and Salt Lake City sights, restaurants, and hotels.

It is my continuing wish to help researchers in the search for their roots. I know that if the research techniques in this work are followed, positive results will occur if the materials needed are available in the Family History Library. I hope you find these techniques as helpful as others have.

Constructive criticisms for improvement of this book are still welcome. Please write me at the publisher's address provided on the copyright page. Good luck and best wishes for successful research!

J. Carlyle Parker
Turlock, California
December 1992

THE FAMILY HISTORY LIBRARY

PREFACE TO FIRST EDITION

The Family History Library in Salt Lake City is the world's largest family history and research library. It has nearly 1.5 million reels of microfilm and over two hundred thousand sheets of microfiche of courthouse, archival, and church records, as well as books and periodicals. The Library's book collection contains over 195,000 volumes and over eight million family group record forms. The scope of the Library's collection is worldwide, with its greatest strength relating to the United States, Canada, and Western Europe.

In some cases it is easier and more economical to do family history and genealogical research in the collection in Salt Lake City than to travel throughout the United States and in foreign countries trying to find the same resources in various county courthouses, churches, local libraries, or cemeteries. It is also easier to research in Salt Lake City than in Denmark, England, and Sweden because in those countries the research sources are not collected in one centralized national archive.

Proper preparation before a visit to the Family History Library in Salt Lake City can save precious time while researching there. It is a waste of time to do some routine tasks at the Family History Library that could have been done at home or at a nearby Family History Center or local public library. A Family History Center is a branch of the Family History Library. Nearly all Family History Centers have microfiche copies of the *International Genealogical Index*, the *Family History Library Catalog*, the *Family Registry*, and the *AIS* (Accelerated Indexing Systems) consolidated indexes to the 1790 through the 1850 United States federal census schedules.

Going to Salt Lake City to Do Family History Research was written as a guide for genealogists preparing to go and use the Family History Library in Salt Lake City, Utah. It addresses the preparation needs of all genealogists from beginners to advanced. It encourages the use of a Family History Center before traveling to Salt Lake City. Genealogists who do not have access to a Family History Center will still find this guide useful as it provides preparation instructions that can be done at home or at local public libraries.

Preface to First Edition

The instructions presented here have been tried and proven valuable to genealogists who enrolled in university courses taught by the author specifically for the purpose of preparing to go to the Family History Library. Those enrolled found that by doing their homework in this manner, in advance, once they arrived at the Library in Salt Lake City they could proceed directly to their most important research materials.

This guide reflects the research viewpoint of its author, who is a veteran of library service, a professional librarian, a genealogist, and the founder and volunteer director for over twenty years of the Modesto California Family History Center. This guide is not an official publication of the Family History Library nor of the Church of Jesus Christ of Latter-day Saints.

I am grateful to the many genealogists who have listened to most of these ideas presented here. I particularly appreciate those who enrolled in my California State University, Stanislaus courses that included a week's research at the Family History Library. They permitted me to experiment on them and confirm that these ideas are effective and productive.

Many individuals helped me in the preparation of *Going to Salt Lake City to Do Family History Research*. I am grateful to the staff of the Family History Library who have assisted me as I have periodically used the Library since 1955 and to A. Gregory Brown and Tom Daniels who provided the Library's photographs and floor plans. Thanks are also extended to Janet G. Parker, Denise Kay Paxton, and Bret H. Parker for their suggestions and proofreading. I also, like millions of genealogists throughout the world, express gratitude to the Church of Jesus Christ of Latter-day Saints for providing the Family History Library and its Family History Centers for people of all denominations to research their family histories.

I am also grateful to the following librarians who responded to my inquiries concerning published and unpublished state-wide indexes of biographical sketches included in chapter 8: Portia Allbert, Kansas State Historical Society, Topeka, Kans.; Lloyd DeWitt Bockstruck, Dallas Public Library; Dallas, Tex.; Donald Brown and John C. Fralish, Jr., State Library of Pennsylvania, Harrisburg, Pa.; John E.

Bye, North Dakota Institute for Regional Studies, North Dakota State University Library, Fargo, N.Dak.; Andrea E. Cantrell, University of Arkansas Libraries, Fayetteville, Ark.; Mary Ann Cleveland, State Library of Florida, Tallahassee, Fla.; David C. Dearborn, New England Historic Genealogical Society, Boston, Mass.; Carol Downey, Arizona Department of Library, Archives and Public Records, Phoenix, Ariz.; Laurel E. Drew, New Mexico State Library, Santa Fe, N.Mex.; Ann Eichinger, South Dakota State Library, Pierre, S.Dak.; Alice Eichholz, Montpelier, Vt.; W. Everard, New Orleans Public Library, New Orleans, La.; P. William Filby, Savage, Md.; Eleanor M. Gehres, Denver Public Library, Denver, Colo.; Peggy Medina Giltrow, New Mexico State Library, Santa Fe, N.Mex.; James L. Hansen, The State Historical Society of Wisconsin, Madison, Wis; Elizabeth P. Jacox, Idaho State Historical Society Library and Archives, Boise, Idaho; Thomas J. Kemp, Pequot Library, Southport, Conn,; Anne Lipscomb, Mississippi State Department of Archives and History, Jackson, Miss.; Kay Littlefield, Bangor Public Library, Bangor, Maine; Virginia H. Ming, The Texas Collection, Baylor University, Waco, Tex.; Tom Muth, Topeka Public Library, Topeka, Kans.; Reidun D. Nuquist, Vermont Historical Society Library, Montpelier, Vt.; Gunther E. Pohl, Great Neck, N.Y.; Wiley R. Pope, Minnesota Historical Society Library, St. Paul, Minn.; Kathryn Ray, District of Columbia Public Library, Washington, D.C.; M. Ann Reinert, Mid-Continent Public Library, Independence, Mo.; Gwen Rice, Wyoming State Library, Cheyenne, Wyo.; Dennis L. Richards, University of Montana Library, Missoula, Mont.; Steve Rodhling, Charleston County Library, Charleston, S.C.; Judy R. Roquet, Oregon State Library, Salem, Oreg.; Stella J. Scheckter, New Hampshire State Library, Concord, N.H.; Linda M. Sommer, South Dakota State Historical Society, Pierre, S.D.; Sandra Stark, Illinois State Historical Library, Springfield, Ill.; Madeleine B. Telfeyan, Rhode Island Historical Society, Providence, R.I.; and Marvin E. Wiggins, Brigham Young University Library, Provo, Utah.

It is my wish to help you in your research. I know that these research techniques work, and I hope you find them as useful as others have. Constructive criticisms for improvement of the guide are welcome. Please write the author at the publisher's address provided on the copyright page. Good luck and best wishes for successful research!

J. Carlyle Parker, Turlock, California, August 1989

INFORMATION BOOK AREA

INTRODUCTION

Before going to the Family History Library in Salt Lake City you should at least read chapters 10, 11, and 12 of this guide. You will be much better prepared if you also complete the steps outlined in chapters 1 and 2. If you have access to a Family History Center, before going to Salt Lake City you should complete as much as you can concerning the preparation suggestions made in chapters 3 through 7.

If a Family History Center is not available to you and you can locate copies of the Library of Congress catalogs mentioned in the "Local Public Library Users" section of chapter 5, it would help you to search them for family histories. The suggested "Additional Reading" at the end of each chapter is very important because the contents and use of some records are not fully explained in this book.

Please bear in mind that you do not have to go to Salt Lake City in order to use the Family History Library. Many researchers use the Family History Library in or near their own home towns through the services of Family History Centers, which serve as branches of the Family History Library. Volunteers are available at Family History Centers to help you use their collections. The Appendix of this work contains a city list of Family History Centers in Canada and the United States. For their locations please call your local Church of Jesus Christ of Latter-day Saints, or write the Family History Library, 35 North West Temple Street, Salt Lake City, Utah 81450 (801) 240-2331.

Microfilm and microfiche may be borrowed for a small service fee through the Family History Library's Family History Centers. Photocopied pages of books and indexes not available in microform may be obtained by mail either through direct correspondence with the Family History Library at the above address or through the use of the "Request for Photocopies" forms available at your local Family History Center.

Introduction

For the convenience of readers, some of the chapters of this guide have been divided into three parts:

    I. Family History Center Users
   II. Local Public Library Users
  III. Home Library Users

These divisions have been made to assist researchers who do not have easy access to a Family History Center or public libraries with genealogical materials.

The guide is written as if all readers were beginners. That, of course, will not be the case. Therefore, some readers will wish to skip parts of the guide that are "old hat" to them. Nevertheless, many genealogical journal book reviewers of the first edition concur that there is something in each chapter for everyone, beginner or advanced. This new edition adds even more information useful for the advanced researcher.

Researchers should bear in mind that not all microforms for foreign countries that appear in the *Family History Library Catalog* are available in the Library. The Library does not have all cataloged microforms for Denmark, England, Finland, Germany, Iceland, Ireland, Netherlands, Norway, Poland, Scotland, Sweden, Switzerland, and Wales. Originals of microforms are stored in the Granite Mountain Records Vault, several miles from the Library. Since copies, not original microforms, are sent to the Library, these films cannot be retrieved at a moment's notice. As microforms are requested, copies are made and then become available for use at the Library.

If you plan to do research concerning foreign countries, it may be important for you to write or call the Library, 35 North West Temple Street, Salt Lake City, Utah 81450 (801) 240-2331, a few weeks ahead of time to check whether they have your desired microfilm numbers in the Library. If they are not available, ask if they can be made available for your date of arrival. Also, provide them with your address and telephone number. Normally, the Library staff will do their best to meet your research needs.

Introduction

Chapters two through seven include some instructions for assisting you in the use of the computer system, *FamilySearch*. Please do not let those instructions intimidate you from using the computer. Most of the Family History Centers and the Family History Library have volunteers who will help you use the various reference tools on *FamilySearch*. If you find the computer instructions in this book too confusing or overwhelming, just forget about them and ask for help from one of the volunteers. You may also wish to try to use *FamilySearch* by reading its menus, search instructions that appear on the screens, or through its help screens. Remember, you are never too old to learn. It is imperative that you use *FamilySearch*, and, just like the "genealogy bug," the "computer bite" will not hurt. You'll find that the two "bugs" are a very good pair. In fact, chances are you'll become an avid computerist.

After you have read and worked through the entire guide, please review the chapter summaries before each visit to the Family History Library.

HOW TO USE THIS GUIDE

THE THREE HOUR APPROACH

If you only have three hours for reading this guide, read the introduction; chapter 10, "What to Take;" chapter 11, "At the Family History Library;" chapter 12, "Miscellaneous Services of the Family History Library"; and the summaries at the end of each chapter.

THE TWO DAY APPROACH

If you only have two days for reading and preparation, besides the above read chapters 1 and 2, which deal with the preparation of pedigrees and family group sheets, and identifying counties or their equivalents in other countries.

THE ONE WEEK APPROACH

If you only have one week for reading and preparation, besides the above read chapter 3 and use the "*International Genealogical Index.*"

THE TWO WEEK APPROACH

If you only have two weeks for reading and preparation, besides the above read chapter 4 and use the "*Ancestral File.*"

THE ONE MONTH APPROACH

If you only have one month for reading and preparation, besides the above read chapter 6 and use the "*Family History Library Catalog: Locality Catalog.*"

How to Use This Guide

THE TWO MONTH APPROACH

If you have two months for reading and preparation, besides the above read chapter 5 concerning finding printed family histories and use the *"Family History Library Catalog: Surname Catalog."*

THE THREE MONTH APPROACH

If you have three months or more for reading and preparation, read the entire guide, and read the country outlines or state outlines of the *United States Research Outline* series in which you're interested. They are available in Family History Centers, or they may be ordered from the Family History Library, 35 North West Temple Street, Salt Lake City, Utah 81450, (801) 240-2331. Do other suggested projects, as needed, and read one of the following how-to-do-it books:

United States (titles for beginners first, advanced last)

Croom, Emily Anne. *Unpuzzling Your Past: A Basic Guide to Genealogy.* 2d ed. White Hall, Va.: Betterway Publications, Inc., 1989.
    FHL GENERAL BOOK AREA 929.1 C888u.

Allen, Desmond Walls, and Billingsley, Carolyn Earle. *Beginner's Guide to Family History Research.* Bountiful, Utah: American Genealogical Lending Library, 1991.
    FHL U.S. & CAN REF AREA 929.1 A53b.

Stryker-Rodda, Harriet. *How to Climb Your Family Tree: Genealogy for Beginners.* Philadelphia: Lippincott, 1977. Reprint. Baltimore: Genealogical Pub. Co., 1983. Large print. Boston: G.K. Hall, 1990.
    FHL GENERAL BOOK AREA 929.1 St89h.

Crandall, Ralph. *Shaking Your Family Tree: A Basic Guide to Tracing Your Family's Genealogy.* Dublin, N.H.: Yankee Publishing, 1988.
    FHL U.S. & CAN REF AREA 929.1 C85s.

Greenwood, Val D. *The Researcher's Guide to American Genealogy.* 2d ed. Baltimore: Genealogical Publishing Co., 1990.
FHL U.S. & CAN REF AREA 973 D27g 1990.

A bibliography of state guides and additional foreign how-to-do-books may be found on pages 49-71 in J. Carlyle Parker's *Library Service for Genealogists*, Gale Genealogy and Local History Series, vol. 15 (Detroit: Gale Research Co., 1981, op. 2d edition in progress by Marietta Publishing Co.).
FHL U.S. & CAN REF AREA 026.9291 P226L.

Foreign Countries and Ethnic Guides (a selected list)

Genealogical Society of the Church of Jesus Christ of Latter-day Saints. *Research Papers.* Salt Lake City, Utah: The Society, 1979-1988.
Many of these papers are available in Family History Centers; now available on microfiche and may be acquired by Family History Centers that do not have paper copies.

Redford, Dorothy Spruill. *Somerset Homecoming: Recovering a Lost Heritage.* New York: Doubleday, 1988. New York: Anchor Books, 1989.
FHL U.S. & CAN BOOK AREA 929.273 L732r.
This work is not considered a how-to-do-it book, but she writes in such detail concerning her African-American family history research that it can be used as such, as well as being very interesting reading.

Rose, James M., & Eichholz, Alice, eds. *Black Genesis.* Gale Genealogy and Local History Series, Vol. 1. Detroit: Gale Research Co., 1978.
FHL U.S. & CAN REF AREA 973 F27r.
A bibliographic guide.

Jonasson, Eric. *The Canadian Genealogical Handbook: A Comprehensive Guide to Finding Your Ancestors in Canada.* 2d ed. rev. and enl. Winnipeg: Wheatfield Press, 1978.
FHL U.S. & CAN REF AREA 971 D27j 1978.

Gardner, David E., and Smith, Frank. *Genealogical Research in England and Wales*. 3 Vols. Salt Lake City: Bookcraft, 1964-1966.
FHL BRITISH REF AREA 929.142 G172g.

Falley, Margaret D. *Irish and Scotch-Irish Ancestral Research: A Guide to the Genealogical Records, Methods and Sources in Ireland*. 2 Vols. Evanston, Ill.: The Author, 1961-62. Reprint. Baltimore: Genealogical Pub. Co., 1981.
FHL BRITISH REF AREA 941.5 D27f.

Hamilton-Edwards, Gerald Kenneth Savery. *In Search of Scottish Ancestry*. 2d ed. Baltimore: Genealogical Pub. Co., 1984.
FHL BRITISH REF AREA 941 D27ham 1984.

Miller, Olga, ed. *Genealogical Research for Czech and Slovak Americans*. Gale Genealogy and Local History Series, Vol. 2. Detroit: Gale Research Co., 1978.
FHL U.S. & CAN REF AREA 943.7 D27m.

Jensen, Larry O. *Genealogical Handbook of German Research*. 2 vols. Pleasant Grove, Utah: The Author, 1978 and 1983. Distributed by Everton Publishers.
FHL EUROPE REF AREA 943 D27j.
Available at Family History Centers: microfiche 6000366-6000368 (v.1 only, 3 microfiches).

Suess, Jared H. *Handy Guide to Hungarian Genealogical Records*. Logan, Utah: Everton Publishers, 1980.
FHL EUROPE BOOK AREA 943.9 D27s.

Kurzweil, Arthur. *From Generation to Generation: How to Trace Your Jewish Genealogy and Personal History*. New York: Morrow, 1980. New York: Schocken Books, 1982.
FHL U.S. & CAN REF AREA 929.1 K967f.
Available from FHL through FHC: microfilm 1059468 Item 4

Platt, Lyman De, ed. *Genealogical-Historical Guide to Latin America.* Gale Genealogy and Local History Series, Vol. 4. Detroit: Gale Research Co., 1978.
FHL LATIN AMERICA REF AREA 980 D27p.

Ryskamp, George R. *Tracing Your Hispanic Heritage.* 1984. Available from Hispanic Family History Research, 4522 Indian Hill, Riverside, CA 92501.
FHL U.S. & CAN REF AREA 946 D27r.

Johansson, Carl-Erik. *Thus They Wrote; A Guide to The Gothic Script of Scandinavia: Denmark, Norway, Finland, Sweden.* Provo, Utah: Brigham Young University Press, 1970.
FHL SCANDINAVIA REF AREA 948 G37j.

Johansson, Carl-Erik. *Cradled in Sweden.* Logan, Utah: Everton Publishers, 1977.
FHL SCANDINAVIA BOOK AREA 948.5 D27j 1972.
    Available from FHL through FHC: microfiche 6030093-6030095 (3 microfiches).

Suess, Jared H. *Handy Guide to Swiss Genealogical Records.* Logan, Utah: Everton Publishers, 1978.
FHL EUROPE REF AREA 949.4 D27s.

A MICROFILM READING AREA

LIST OF ABBREVIATIONS

AIS	Accelerated Indexing Systems
CAN	Canada
FGRC	*Family Group Records Collection*
FHCs	Family History Centers of the Family History Library of the Church of Jesus Christ of Latter-day Saints
FHL	Family History Library of the Church of Jesus Christ of Latter-day Saints, Salt Lake City, Utah
FHLC	*Family History Library Catalog*
FICHE	Microfiche
FILM	Microfilm
GSU	Genealogical Society of Utah
IGI	*International Genealogical Index*
II	Interval International Resort
n.p.	No publisher
op	Out-of-print
PAF	*Personal Ancestral File*
Q	Oversize
RCI	Resort Condominiums International
REF	Reference
REG	Register
SASE	Self-addressed, stamped envelope
s.l.	Without place of publication
TIB	*Temple Records Index Bureau*

PART I

BEFORE YOU GO

Chapter 1

START WITH YOURSELF

Starting with yourself prepare a pedigree chart and family group sheet.
Write down the dates and places of births, marriages, and deaths,
where appropriate. Some pedigree charts and family group charts
should be started before going to either the Family History Library or a
Family History Center. Women's maiden names, instead of their
married names, are used on pedigrees and family group sheets.

Work from what you know or have in your personal papers to the
unknown. You should not start with a famous person with your
surname and research his or her descendants. Such research can
mislead you and waste a lot of time searching family lines that may not
be your direct line.

Inquire at your local library or call a Church of Jesus Christ of Latter-
day Saints to find out where you can obtain blank pedigree and family
group forms. The following firms are a few among many that provide
mail order service for genealogical supplies:

> Everton Publishers, Inc., P.O. Box 368, Logan, UT 84321,
> (801) 752-6022
>
> Genealogy Unlimited, Inc., 789 South Buffalo Grove Road,
> Buffalo Grove, IL 60089, (800) 666-4363
>
> Genealogical Books in Print, 6818 Lois Drive, Springfield, VA
> 22150, (703) 971-5877
>
> Hearthstone Bookshop, Potomac Square, 8405-H Richmond
> Highway, Alexandria, VA 22309, (703) 360-6900
>
> Genealogy Plus, General Delivery, Langdon, Alberta, Canada
> T0J 1X0, (403) 936-5386.
>
> S.E.L. Enterprises, 178 Grandview Avenue, Thornhill,
> Ontario, Canada L3T 1J1, (416) 889-0498

Sample Pedigree Chart

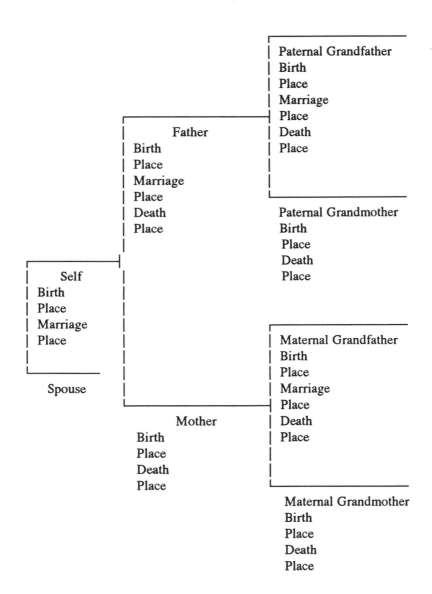

Personal papers that are the most useful in supplying data for the pedigree and family group charts are

baby books	journals
certificates	letters
citizenship papers	military records
deeds	newspaper clippings
diaries	probates
family Bibles	wills
funeral memorial cards	

PREPARE A LIST OF RESEARCH NEEDS

From the blank spaces on your pedigree and family group charts prepare a list of research needs of interest. Rank them in priority order to follow while at the library, including which family or families you wish to research first. Include the geographical places involved with these needs, objectives, and priorities. Faithful adherence to such lists may save you from the distractions that might otherwise sidetrack you from your primary goals. You should also regularly ask yourself, "Is this part of my research really necessary to achieve my goals?"

If you have a personal computer it may be more efficient to prepare a list of research needs on it, instead of the below typed or hand written cards. The inventory programs of the *Personal Ancestral File* (*PAF*) can assist in some aspects of the above lists. The *PAF* is an excellent computer program for family history research, and very reasonably priced. It is available from the Church of Jesus Christ of Latter-day Saints, Salt Lake Distribution Center, 1956 West 1700 South, Salt Lake City, Utah 84065, order desk telephone number (800) 537-5950.

Chapter 1

Sample List of Research Needs in Priority Order

Names, places and dates of birth and death
of the two daughters of John Black Greer, perhaps
born in Glasgow, Scotland. Both died about 1850
under 8 years of age, perhaps St. Louis, Missouri.

Birth place of John Black Greer, perhaps
Ireland. Married Jean Leishman, 23 August 1856,
Binghamton, Broome, New York. Father of Jane
Greer Parkinson.

Birth date of John Parkinson, born Linn Co.,
Ohio, father of David, born 3 May 1871, Jefferson
Co., Iowa.

The addresses and telephone numbers of the leaders of *PAF* user groups
are available at Family History Centers or from the Family History
Library, 35 North West Temple Street, Salt Lake City, Utah 84150,
(801) 240-2331 (7:45-4:30 p.m., Monday - Friday). A helpful
keyboard template for MS-DOS version of the *PAF* is available from
Kathy Cook Consulting, P.O. Box 393, Escondido CA 92015.
Included with the template is a pocket key dictionary of *PAF*
commands. An excellent supplementary *PAF* user's manual is Joan
Lowrey's *Personal Ancestral File 2.2 Users Guide*, 4th ed. (La Jolla,
Calif.: Joan Lowrey Enterprises (7371 Rue Michael, 92037), 1990,
FHL GENERAL BOOK AREA 005.3 L955).

Research objectives may also be prepared through the use of the notes
mode of the *PAF*. Many other supportive utility programs for *PAF* are
announced, questions answered, bulletin board systems and tips
provided in the *International PAF Users' Group Quarterly*, 2463
Ledgewood Drive, West Jordan, UT 84084-5738.

The *PAF* and other computer software for genealogical computing are nicely explained in Donna Przech and Joan Lowrey's *A Guide to Selecting Genealogy Software* (La Jolla, Calif.: Joan Lowrey Enterprises, 1991, FHL in process) and Paul A. Anderick and Richard A. Pence's *Computer Genealogy: A Guide to Research Through High Technology* (Rev. ed., Salt Lake City: Ancestry, 1991, FHL GENERAL BOOK AREA 929.10285 An22c 1991).

PREPARE A LIST OF INDIVIDUALS

Prepare a list of individuals for whom you hope to find information. It is more practical to write each name on a 3"x5" card. You may wish to limit individual cards to the last known ancestors on your pedigree. Put the surname in the upper left-hand corner of the card, followed by the first and middle names and some vital data below the name. Information should also include the name of the spouse and the child who is in the direct line being researched.

Sample Individual's Card

Greer, John Black

    b. perhaps in Glasgow, Scotland
    m. Jean Leishman, 23 August 1856, Binghamton, Broome, New York
    d. Cleveland, Cuyahoga, Ohio
    f. of Jane Greer, wife of Timothy Parkinson

PREPARE FAMILY SURNAME CARDS

Prepare a 3"x5" card or a computer entry for each family surname for which you would like to research and find a printed family history. Write the family's surname near the upper left-hand corner of the card.

Chapter 1

Under the surname write the names of prominent members of the family, the dates and places important in their lives, and their professions or other relevant information, such as outstanding accomplishments or service.

Sample Family Surname Card

Parkinson Family
  Parkinson, John
   born Linn Co., Ohio
   father of David
   born 3 May 1871
   Jefferson Co. Iowa
   Doctor

PREPARE A LIST OF GEOGRAPHICAL LOCATIONS

The final set of 3"x5" cards or computer lists that you should prepare is for each geographical location of research interest. Geographical cards or computer lists should contain in the upper left-hand corner the name of the state, the county, and the town or the name of the foreign country, the county, and the parish, village, or town, if known. Below the geographical location list the full names of some of the ancestors who lived there or the names of prominent members of the family, their occupations, if known, the years they lived there, and vital dates.

Sample Geographical Location Card

Ohio, Linn Co.

   Parkinson, John
    born Linn Co., Ohio
    father of David
    born 3 May 1871
    Jefferson Co. Iowa
    Doctor

At this point you should have prepared four different sets of cards or lists: research needs in priority order, individuals, family surnames, and geographical locations. These will be used in many different ways and will prove helpful in the research strategies explained later in this book.

After you have collected and organized the data found in your home, write or call relatives who may have done some genealogical research or have papers concerning your ancestors. Inquire whether they have pedigree charts or family group sheets that you can use to extend your ancestral lines. Also ask if they know of any printed biographical sketches, family histories or manuscript histories that include your ancestors.

You should keep copies of all of your correspondence. Some researchers find it useful to keep a "Correspondence Log" and a "Research Log" listing all of their correspondence and research, similar to the following:

Sample Correspondence Log

Date	Letter to	Subject	Date Rec'd Answer
1/3/92	Emily Smith	Place of marriage of Jane Greer	2/23/92

Chapter 1

Sample Research Log

Library	Source	Call #	Page in File	Date
FHL	1850 Census Elk Co. Penn.	444744	7	5/2/92

The research log can become the table of contents to your note file if you number your notes. Other researchers simply file their correspondence together with research notes in file folders under family surnames.

ADDITIONAL READING:

Stryker-Rodda, Harriet. "Beginning With Yourself," chapter 1, pages 13-25; and "Keeping Records," chapter 2, pages 26-42. In *How to Climb Your Family Tree: Genealogy for Beginners*. Philadelphia: J. B. Lippincott, 1977.
> FHL GENERAL BOOK AREA 929.1 St89h.

SUMMARY:

Prepare pedigrees, family group sheets, and cards or lists of families, individuals, geographical locations, and ancestral research needs in priority order. Write or call relatives for additional family history information.

"Do you think that the Personal Ancestral File could handle my llamas' pedigrees?"
> -- 1990 telephone question to author

8

Chapter 2

IDENTIFY COUNTIES

Because the majority of the records that relate to family history research are housed in county court houses (New England towns and some foreign countries are the exceptions), it is necessary to identify the county (or equivalent for foreign countries) for every place where the ancestors you wish to research were born, married, and died. It is also helpful to know the counties where they lived in the United States during the census years of 1790, 1800, 1810, 1820, 1830, 1840, 1850, 1860, 1870, 1880, 1900, 1910, or 1920.

The geographical cards or lists outlined in chapter 1 can be used in the steps below to identify counties. County names (or equivalent), once identified, should be added to the geographical cards and to all geographical entries on pedigrees and family group sheets.

I. FAMILY HISTORY CENTER USERS:

One easy way to identify counties is by using the *Family History Library Catalog: Locality Catalog.* Consult the first few left-hand columns on the first microfiche of the state (or several microfiche for some countries) of the *Family History Library Catalog: Locality Catalog* and search for the name of the city or cities for which you need county names. County names (or equivalent) are given for all cities for which the Family History Library has materials.

Sample
Family History Library Catalog: Locality Catalog
Geographical Entry on Microfiche

Warsaw, Missouri -----> Missouri, Benton, Warsaw

Chapter 2

This catalog is available also on the CD-ROM computer system, *FamilySearch*. The microfiche edition is available in all Family History Centers. *FamilySearch* is available in most Family History Centers, the Family History Library, and will be available in 1993 in the *FamilySearch* Center in the historic Hotel Utah building, South Temple and Main Streets.

If your Family History Center has *FamilySearch*, you may want to search for the names of your counties on it by looking at the "Locality Browse." To get to "Locality Browse" choose (select) in the following order:

"Family History Library Catalog" from the FAMILYSEARCH MAIN MENU by placing the bar over the "Family History Library Catalog" line with the down arrow and by **pressing "Enter."**

"Locality Browse" from the LIBRARY CATALOG MAIN MENU by **pressing "Enter."**

"Town and parish list" from the LOCALITY BROWSE screen.

Press "Enter," type the name of the city of interest, press "Enter."

In a few seconds the name of the city, county, and state may be highlighted on the screen or you may need to read down the screen or press the page down key (PgDn) until you see your city and state, then make a note of the county's name. Press "F11" and continue your search for the second city by repeating the steps from selecting "Locality Browse" as explained above.

If a city is not listed in the *Family History Library Catalog: Locality Catalog*, the Family History Library does not have materials cataloged under that city. However, the Library may have something cataloged for that city under the name of its county, and you may have to wait until you can consult the sources mentioned in Parts II and III of this chapter to determine the name of the county.

The Family History Center may also have the following source, which you should check for those places not found in the *Family History Library Catalog: Locality Catalog*: *Bullinger's Postal & Shippers Guide for the United States & Canada: Containing Post Offices & Railroad Stations, With the Railroad or Steamer Line on Which Every Place or the Nearest Communicating Point is Located, and the List of Railroads & Water Lines With Their Terminal Points* (Westwood, N.J.: Bullinger's Guides, 1878, 1895, 1951, or 1961; FHL microfilm numbers: FHL U.S. & CAN FILM AREA 1961 - 1320793 Item 7, 1951 - 483709, 1895 - 1033518, 1878 - 1002373 Item 2). If you need to use it when you get to the Family History Library, it is in both the reference and the regular collections, with the call number: FHL U.S. & CAN BOOK AREA 970 E8b.

For those really tough places to find, such as ghost towns or places that no longer exist and are not listed in available reference sources, a letter to the state library or the historical society library of the state involved may bring the needed answer. Most of those libraries maintain collections or card files for answering such difficult questions. Most public libraries can provide the state libraries' and state historical society libraries' addresses from the *American Library Directory, 1992-93*, 2 vols., 45th ed. (New Providence, N.J.: R. R. Bowker, 1992, FHL U.S. & CAN REF AREA 973 J54a).

FOREIGN PLACE NAMES

Many of the Family History Centers have an excellent atlas with a detailed list of English parishes, *The Phillimore Atlas and Index of Parish Registers* (Chichester, England: Phillimore, 1984, FHL BRITISH REF AREA 942 E7pa). Most specific how-to-do-it books for foreign countries explain the use of that country's gazetteers and postal guides in genealogical research. The Family History Library also has atlases, gazetteers, and postal directories for many foreign countries to assist with place identification. Many of these are in microform and may be found in some Family History Centers or may be ordered. For those not available in microform you may have to wait until you go to Salt Lake City to gain access to them.

Chapter 2

The Subject headings under which they will be found in the *Family History Library Catalog: Locality Catalog* are as follows:

Gazetteers: FRANCE - GAZETTEERS

Geographical Names: FRANCE - NAMES, GEOGRAPHICAL

Ghost Towns: FRANCE - HISTORICAL GEOGRAPHY
                     FRANCE - HISTORY

Post Offices: FRANCE - POSTAL AND SHIPPING
                     GUIDES

COUNTY BOUNDARY CHANGES

As your research progresses you may find that you must learn something about county boundaries. You may be researching for ancestors in a particular county and find that the *Family History Library Catalog: Locality Catalog* only lists records for the county back to 1851. At this point you need to know what county or counties are the parent counties. In order to determine this you need to use one or both of the following:

Everton, George B., ed. *The Handy Book for Genealogists.* 8th ed., rev. and enl. Logan, Utah: Everton Publishers, 1991.
    FHL U.S. & CAN REF AREA 973 D27e 1991.

Ancestry's Red Book: American State, County, and Town Sources. Edited by Alice Eichholz. Rev. ed. Salt Lake City: Ancestry Publishing, 1992.
    FHL U.S. & CAN REF AREA 973 D27rb.

The above works are usually the best single sources to answer the problem of county boundaries. However, their information is limited to the date of the county's creation and names of the county or counties from which it was formed. You may need additional assistance concerning difficult county boundary problems. A few states have prepared detailed books on the subject. These books and references to parts of other sources are listed in "A Selected Bibliography of Statewide Place Name Literature, Old Gazetteers, Postal Service Histories, Ghost Town Directories and Histories, and Boundary Change Guides," in *Library Service for Genealogists*, ed. J. Carlyle Parker, Gale Genealogy and Local History Series, vol. 15 (Detroit: Gale Research Co., 1981, op, FHL U.S. & CAN REF AREA 026.9291 P226L, 2d edition in progress by Marietta Publishing Co.), pages 29-47.

Many county histories also include boundary change information, as well as township boundary changes. For problems that can not be resolved through the above sources, you should write the county clerk of the county involved and ask for assistance.

Sample subject headings used in the *Family History Library Catalog - Locality Catalog* relative to sources that identify county boundaries:

> CALIFORNIA - LAND AND PROPERTY - HISTORY
> KANSAS - HISTORICAL GEOGRAPHY

TOWNSHIPS

Some researchers may need to identify the county for a named township, such as Washington Township, Ohio. John L. Andriot compiled *Township Atlas of the United States, Named Townships* (McLean, Va: Andriot Associates, 1977, FHL U.S. & CAN REF AREA 973 E7an 1987. Microfiche. Salt Lake City: GSU, 1989. 12 microfiches. FHL U.S. & CAN FICHE AREA 6049121). It is the most useful reference source for assisting with named township problems. This atlas contains current outline maps for the twenty-two states with named townships, showing the names and locations of counties, and county maps showing the names and locations of their named townships and other minor civil divisions. The 223-page index contains entries for over 52,000 counties, districts, divisions, gores, grants, named precincts, plantations, towns, townships, and others.

Chapter 2

There is a newer atlas by Andriot, *Township Atlas of the United States* (McLean, Va: Andriot Associates, 1979) for all townships for all states. However, it is not as detailed as the 1977 atlas for the twenty-two states with named townships.

If more information is needed concerning townships, you can turn to the county histories of the county concerned. Some county histories include a history of the townships and often explain their boundaries.

II. LOCAL PUBLIC LIBRARY USERS:

For county names in the United States check the indexes of the Rand, McNally and Co., *Commercial Atlas & Marketing Guide* (Chicago: 67th- 1936-). For counties or regional subdivisions in other countries check *Webster's Geographical Dictionary* or the *Columbia Lippincott Gazetteer*. For any cities not found in these sources you will have to check other atlases or maps that may be available at the public library. You may have to wait until you arrive at the Family History Library to check the place names not found.

III. HOME LIBRARY USERS:

Many counties can be determined through the use of maps or atlases that you have collected and have at home. The *National Five-Digit Zip Code & Post Office Directory*, which is available at your local post office, gives counties for all cities listed at the beginning of each state's listing.

If any of the above sources do not identify the county of a city which you need to research, you may also write the State Library of the state for which you have a problem place name and enlist their assistance in determining the county. The addresses of State Libraries are in the *American Library Directory* at your local library, or simply address your letter to the Reference Department, State Library, and the capital city and state.

ADDITIONAL READING:

Parker, J. Carlyle. "Identifying the Counties for Cities," chapter 5, pages 25-48. In *Library Service for Genealogists*. Gale Genealogy and Local History Series, vol. 15. Detroit: Gale Research Co., 1981, op. 2d edition in progress by Marietta Publishing Co.
FHL U.S. & CAN REF AREA 026.9291 P226L.

SUMMARY:

You must know the counties for all cities where ancestors were born, married, or died. Check maps and atlases at home, or the *Family History Library Catalog: Locality Catalog*, Rand McNally's *Commercial Atlas & Marketing Guide*, or the *National Five-Digit Zip Code & Post Office Directory* (2 vols., Washington, D.C.: U.S. Postal Service, 1992).

Q. "Where is Dover, California?"

A. "This little village was started in 1866 and at one time attracted considerable attention. It was situated on the San Joaquin River, above the mouth of the Merced River."
    -- *History of Merced County, California*. San
       Francisco: Elliott & Moore, 1881, page 118.

A Merced County, California dock town for shipping winter wheat by steamer via the San Joaquin River to San Francisco (about 130 miles). Now, a cornfield.
                                                            -- The author

FamilySearch COMPUTERS

Chapter 3

INTERNATIONAL GENEALOGICAL INDEX

It is very important that a survey be made to determine what research has already been completed. It is a waste of time to launch into in-depth research without attempting to determine what has been done by other researchers. One of the first sources that should be consulted is the *International Genealogical Index (IGI)*.

The *International Genealogical Index* is available in all Family History Centers and will be available in 1993 in the *FamilySearch* Center in the historic Hotel Utah building. A few public and several genealogical libraries have also purchased the *International Genealogical Index*. However, you may have to wait until you arrive at the Family History Library. Microfiche copies and the *FamilySearch* edition of the *IGI* on floors of the Library other than the Main floor only include the countries represented on that floor.

The latest edition of the *IGI*, 1992, contains 187 million name entries. It is the largest and most useful genealogical index available. Its entries cover deceased persons primarily born between the early 1500's and the present.

The *IGI* is on microfiche and on *FamilySearch*. It consists of research submitted by LDS Church members or entered from the Church's Name Extraction Program since October 1969, including many pre-1969 records that have been added by the Church. It is international in scope and based on government, church, and personal records. However, it contains more names for Denmark, England, Finland, Germany, Iceland, Mexico, Netherlands, Norway, Scotland, Sweden, Switzerland, United States, and Wales than for other countries.

The two versions of the *IGI* are usually not released simultaneously; therefore you should check the dates of each and use the latest release or edition. The date for the *IGI* microfiche is printed at the top of each microfiche. The date for the *FamilySearch IGI* appears on the program's first screen. As you make notes about ancestors found in the

Chapter 3

IGI, make sure that you also record the year that the *IGI* was published. Names in the *IGI* on microfiche are arranged alphabetically within each state where a vital event took place for the United States and Mexico; each province of Canada; the counties of Denmark, England, Finland, Norway, Scotland, Sweden, and Wales; and by country for each of the other countries of the world. It is primarily useful for finding records of births or christenings and marriages. There are some death records included and some record entries based on the U.S. census schedules. The entries for Denmark, Finland, Iceland, Norway, Sweden, and Wales are listed separately by given names and by surnames (two alphabets for each country).

For checking the *IGI*, use the 3"x5" cards prepared in chapter 1 for individuals and select the ancestors for whom you wish to search. A search should include at least the last known ancestors on your pedigree. Each ancestor searched should be checked in the *IGI* under the state (province, county, or country) of birth and state (province, county, or country) of marriage. The surnames at the top of the microfiche, that can be read without a microfiche reader, are the first and last surnames that appear in the text of the microfiche.

Sample *International Genealogical Index* Entries

KENTUCKY

Vinson, Alexander Lucy Gibson H M 13 Sep 1817 Christian
                                Hopkinsville 7128123 96

Vinson, Benjamin Alexander Vinson/Lucy Gibson M B 29 Feb
                        1824 Muhlenberg   7802625 97

The first sample above is an entry for the marriage ("M") of Alexander Vinson (the husband, "H") to Lucy Gibson on September 13, 1817 in Hopkinsville, Christian County, Kentucky. The second sample is an entry for the birth ("B") of a male ("M"), Benjamin Vinson, to parents Alexander Vinson and Lucy Gibson in Muhlenberg County, Kentucky, February 29, 1824. Abbreviations like H, M, and B, as in the examples above, are explained at the top and bottom of the second and third columns respectively. If you are unable to understand *IGI* entries, ask a Family History Library or Family History Center volunteer to help you interpret them.

When using the *IGI*, record all of the information except for post-1970 dates in the columns labeled "b", "e", and "s." Those columns relate to the temple work done by members of the Church of Jesus Christ of Latter-day Saints and should be noted by LDS members. The reason that LDS members submit names of deceased relatives for temple work is because they believe that all persons should be provided the opportunity to be baptized by immersion, married for eternity, and to receive additional religious ordinances that have to be done on earth. Latter-day Saints believe that these ordinances can be done by proxy in the Church's temples by living persons, for the deceased, who then have the choice and freedom to accept or reject these ordinances in the spirit life beyond the grave.

The numbers in the last two columns of the *IGI* are the "Batch Number" and "Serial Sheet" number. Record these numbers in order to find the source of the *IGI* information: the patron's form on the batch microfilm or the microfilm or book number from which the genealogical information was extracted. The patron's form contains the name and address of the person or patron who submitted the data and a reference to the source of the data. It may be useful in some cases to consult the source used to submit the data.

In order to obtain the name and address of the person who submitted a name that has been indexed in the *IGI*, check the batch number in the next-to-last column of each entry. Patron-submitted names are identified by batch numbers wherein the first two digits represent the year of submission (7234444), with the following exceptions:

694, 725, 744, 745. 754, and 766

The names of persons who having submitted names after May 1991 are

not reported in any way. The person who submitted a common
ancestor may not be a direct relative, because in some circumstances
Church members are permitted to submit names for all persons with the
same surname as an ancestor of theirs within a ten-mile radius of that
ancestor's residence or within the same county in the United States
where that ancestor resided.

The patron's forms are microfilmed and the paper copy is destroyed.
The microfilm number of the microfilmed patron's form is listed as the
"Input Source" on the microfiche copy of the *IGI Batch Number Index*,
opposite the batch number. The *IGI Batch Number Index* is a small,
separate microfiche publication, usually filed with or near the *IGI*.

Sample *IGI Batch Number Index* Entry on Microfiche

BATCH NUMBER	INPUT SOURCE
7200322	820079
7200323	820068

The serial sheet number is used like a page number to locate the exact
patron's record within the batch number on the microfilm.

There are three ways to access a patron-submitted record, but in any
case you must determine the microfilm number for the submitted
record. The "Input Source" may be checked while researching at the
Family History Library, or beforehand, by requesting a photocopy via
the Library's "Request for Photocopies" form, or by ordering the
microfilm through the Family History Center's interlibrary loan
program.

The majority of the entries in the *IGI* are not patron-submitted but were
extracted from vital and parish records by LDS Church volunteers.
The sources used for entries that are not patron-submitted may also be

found on the *IGI Batch Number Index*. It lists some printouts of records. The printouts contain the same information found in the *IGI*. However, if you would like to use an alphabetical list of a single record or part of a record, it may be useful to use a printout microfilm.

Another useful supplement to the *IGI* for determining what records have been extracted is the *Parish and Vital Records List*. It is also a small microfiche publication and is arranged in alphabetical order by country and sub-arranged by state or province and county. It provides the years extracted from each type of record; the Family History Library call number for the microfilm or book used; and, for a few records, a microfilm number for a computer print-out of a listing, in alphabetical order, of the names extracted. It is available at the Family History Library, Family History Centers, and it will be available in 1993 in the *FamilySearch* Center in the historic Hotel Utah building, South Temple and Main Streets.

Sample *Parish and Vital Records List* Entry on Microfiche

UNITED STATES
MAINE

CO.   TOWN/   PERIOD RECD PRINTOUT PROJECT SOURCE
       PARISH FROM-TO TYPE CALL NO.

ANDRSC TURNER 1776-1875 BIR 0883819 C50327-1 012262

The *IGI* batch numbers that start with the letter "A" with sealing ("s") dates between 1942 and 1970 may be traced through the Archive (main) Section of the *Family Group Records Collection* (*FGRC* listed in the source column of the *IGI* as "AR REC"). The person who submitted the data may no longer be available; however, the form will contain other useful information. The *Family Group Records Collection* is explained in chapter 11.

Chapter 3

The *IGI* batch numbers T000001 through T000010, and T000150- may also be traced to the *Family Group Records Collection.*

Occasionally the word "FILM" is given in the serial sheet column, in which case a microform number will be provided in the batch number. Some entries now include the symbols "∆ ," "#," "∂," and ">." The "∆ " stands for "Entry altered from source" (after evaluation for clearer meaning); and the "#," "∂," and ">" represent "Relative named in source." The symbol "#" also identifies that the names of parents or grandparents are included; also "∂" that some dates may have been estimated; and ">" that additional information is only available to direct descendants of the person listed in the *IGI* from Special Services, Temple Department, 50 East North Temple Street, Salt Lake City, Utah 84150.

IGI ON *FAMILYSEARCH*

The *IGI* is available also on the CD-ROM computer system, *FamilySearch.* The microfiche edition is available in all Family History Centers. *FamilySearch* is available in most Family History Centers, the Family History Library, and will be available in 1993 in the *FamilySearch* Center in the historic Hotel Utah building. The Centers and the Library have volunteers who will help you with the computer.

If your Family History Center has *FamilySearch*, you may want to search for the names of your ancestors on it by making the following choices (selections):

"International Genealogical Index" from the FAMILYSEARCH MAIN MENU by placing the bar over the "International Genealogical Index" line with the down arrow and by **pressing "Enter."**

"Press F4 to begin a search" at the *International Genealogical Index* screen.

At the SELECT REGION OF THE WORLD TO SEARCH screen **move the bar down, with the arrow key, to the desired country and press "Enter."**

At the SEARCH MENU the bar covers the "SIMILAR surnames (last name) spelling search" under the "BIRTH AND MARRIAGE INDEX." You may move the bar to several other selections. However, you may find it most useful to search for a person using the **"SIMILAR surnames (last name) spelling search"**, rather than the "EXACT surname spelling search" under either "BIRTH AND MARRIAGE INDEX" or "PARENT INDEX." The "SIMILAR surnames (last name) spelling search" choice provides you with the opportunity to find other spellings of your ancestral names. The next *FamilySearch* edition will provide the separation of birth and marriage entries.

The next screen will ask first for the "Given Name(s)"; **type in given name(s) and press "Enter."** The typing area bar will advance to the "Surname," at which you must **type in the surname and press "Enter."** The type area bar will advance to the "Year of Event (birth, christening, marriage, will, etc.)." **If you know the date, type it in.** If you do not know the date, you should estimate it and **press "Enter."** It is best not to use the "F10=Filter" option, as it slows a search for a specific individual.

Press either "F12=Start Search" or "Enter."

Closely follow the screen directions for inserting and ejecting the "disc," which you leave in its case for placing in the disc drive.

When going on to **a new search press "F4."** Press the type of search and pay attention to the OPTIONS, "Begin a new search" or "Modify previous search." If the next person you are searching has the same surname, it is faster to move the bar down to "Modify previous search" and press "Enter." Type in the new given name(s), hit the space bar to erase any unwanted letters that may follow the name(s) typed and press either "F12" or "Enter."

To print a name press "F2." The PRINT OPTIONS warn you that printing the source(s) takes extra time. You need the source(s), so follow the screen instructions for printing them, keeping in mind the time elements of the warning. If you wish to consult the source to see if the person who submitted the data may be able to assist you in your research, order the input source microfilm or submit a "Request for

Chapter 3

Photocopies" order form for a copy of the patron-submitted form. If the data is not patron-submitted, you may wish to order the input source in order to read possible additional data from the input source that was not extracted, such as notes about your ancestor or burial data.

Researchers with computers with genealogical software that can receive GEDCOM data may download to their preformated disks, in all sizes, any printable data from the *IGI* by following the prompts for preparing a "HOLDING FILE."

Remember, it is faster to do an *IGI* search with the microfiche edition than with *FamilySearch*.

I. FAMILY HISTORY CENTER USERS:

The *International Genealogical Index* is on microfiche and *FamilySearch* available at the Family History Library, the Family History Centers, and will be available in 1993 in the *FamilySearch* Center in the historic Hotel Utah building, South Temple and Main Streets.

II. LOCAL PUBLIC LIBRARY USERS:

Some public and genealogical libraries have purchased the *IGI*. Make sure that you check it and record its copyright date.

III. HOME LIBRARY USERS:

If you are impatient you can hire the *IGI* consulted by mail through the services of many of the genealogists who advertise in the *Genealogical Helper* or other genealogical magazines. However, that should not be necessary since my hope is that you'll be in Salt Lake City soon. Copies of the microfiche and *FamilySearch* editions of the *IGI* are available on the Main Floor of the Family History Library and will be available in 1993 in the *FamilySearch* Center in the historic Hotel Utah building, South Temple and Main Streets. Microfiche copies and the *FamilySearch* edition of the *IGI* on the other floors of the Library only include the countries represented on that floor.

Individuals may also purchase parts of the *IGI* on microfiche for non-commercial use. Write the Family History Library, 35 North West Temple Street, Salt Lake City, UT 84150.

ADDITIONAL READING:

Additional information concerning the *IGI*'s use is found in the following Research Outlines and pamphlet which are available at the Family History Library and Family History Centers:

International Genealogical Index (on microfiche). 2d ed. Research Outline Series IGI, No. 1. Salt Lake City: Corporation of the President of The Church of Jesus Christ of Latter-day Saints, 1992. 4 pages.

International Genealogical Index (on compact disc). Research Outline Series IGI, No. 5. 3d ed. Salt Lake City: Corporation of the President of The Church of Jesus Christ of Latter-day Saints, 1990. 4 pages.

Finding an IGI Source. 2d ed. Research Outline Series IGI, No. 2. Salt Lake City: Corporation of the President of The Church of Jesus Christ of Latter-day Saints, 1992. 4 pages.

Parish and Vital Records Computer Printout. Research Outline Series IGI, No. 4. Salt Lake City: Corporation of the President of The Church of Jesus Christ of Latter-day Saints, 1988.

"FamilySearch: International Genealogical Index (on compact disc) Getting Started."* 2d ed. Salt Lake City: Corporation of the President of The Church Jesus Christ of Latter-day Saints, 1990. 20 pages. In *"FamilySearch"* [manuals in binder].

For researchers who do not have access to a Family History Center, an excellent article about the *IGI* is Elizabeth L. Nichols' "The *International Genealogical Index,"* *The New England Historical and*

Chapter 3

Genealogical Register 137 (July 1983): 193-209, FHL GENERAL BOOK AREA 929.3 N515i. There is updated information in her more recent article, "*International Genealogical Index (IGI)* 1988 Edition is Distributed to Family History Centers," *Genealogical Helper* 42 (September/October 1988): 5-9.

SUMMARY:

Check the *International Genealogical Index* for all of the ancestors for whom you wish to do research under the geographical location of their birth and marriage. Not everyone will find their ancestors indexed. However, such a large percentage of researchers do find completed research in the *IGI* that it is imperative that the search be made. Many skeptical researchers have been amazed to find, through the use of the *IGI*, that someone else has worked on their ancestral lines.

"This stuff [the *IGI*] can give you a real high!"

-- Hippie researcher, Modesto California
Family History Center, early 1970's

Chapter 4

ANCESTRAL FILE

Another step to take in the survey of completed research is to consult
FamilySearch's *Ancestral File*. Your individual and family surname
3"x5" cards or your lists may be used in a search of any of these
sources. The largest of these indexes is the *Ancestral File*.

The *Ancestral File* is only available on *FamilySearch* at the Family
History Library, most Family History Centers, and a few public and
genealogical libraries. It will be available in 1993 in the *FamilySearch*
Center in the historic Hotel Utah building, South Temple and Main
Streets. You should search it for the names of your ancestors, as it is
another way of determining what research has already been done
concerning your families and finding the names and addresses of
possible relations who have done and submitted the research data,
starting in 1979. It contains approximately thirteen million names.
Other than for corrections and minor additions, the file has no
documentation, although submitters' names and addresses are given.
The *Ancestral File* has submission, as well as computer input, errors.

The *Ancestral File* is a computer data base which started with
contributions of four generations of ancestors by members of the
Church of Jesus Christ of Latter-day Saints. Data is still being added to
this data base. The *Ancestral File* has expanded far beyond four
generations, and the Family History Library encourages all researchers
to contribute their pedigrees and family group sheets for inclusion in it.

To use the *Ancestral File* make the following choices (selections) in
order, or ask a volunteer for help:

"Ancestral File" from the FAMILYSEARCH MAIN MENU by
placing the bar over the "Ancestral File" line with the down arrow and
by **pressing "Enter."**

Please record the date of the edition that appears on the *Ancestral File*
screen.

Chapter 4

Next press "F4=Search" at the ANCESTRAL FILE window screen, which will begin your search.

Press "Enter" for "By SIMILAR last name spelling" at the SEARCH window, as it is faster and will also inform you of variant spellings which you should learn from it.

Type the first and middle names (example: Mary Ann) in the colored bar labeled, "Given Name(s)" on the "Ancestor's name:" line of the SEARCH BY SURNAME AND GIVEN NAME screen. **Press "Enter."**

The colored bar will move to the "Surname (Last Name)." **Type in the name** and press **"Enter."**

The bar is now in the "Birth Year:" and if you know the year of birth of your ancestor, type it in, as it speeds up the search. Press "Enter" **or "F12=Begin Search."** If you do not know the date press "Enter" or "F12=Begin Search."

If the person you are searching is in the *Ancestral File*, the name will appear on the screen highlighted with the bar; if not, the highlight bar will appear over a similar name. At this point you have the following numbered options:

1. "Enter=Details." This selection will produce a window with the name of the person and various data concerning him or her; date of birth or "LIVING," if not deceased at the time of the record submission; marriage date; sex; AFN (*Ancestral File* number); names of father, mother, and spouse (often just "LIVING," if that is the case at the time of record submission). Information concerning living persons is very limited and restricted by the program in order to protect their privacy rights.

Another press of the **"Enter"** will bring up more details about the individual. However, you may be directed to CHANGE COMPACT DISCS. Follow those instructions to the letter. After the computer ejects the disc currently in the CD-ROM, replace it with the one requested. The computer takes some time to read the new disc, followed by a **"PLEASE WAIT"** window, as if it knows you may be too excited to wait for the results. WAIT! Pressing other keys to push it along faster will just get you into a time-consuming mess. The detailed window adds information for christening, death, burial, and the names of all spouses. At this window pressing "F9" will bring up source information, which usually provides the name and address of the person or persons submitting the data, including the microfilm number of data microfilmed; research interest; the names of related family organizations; and notes and history of changes in the records, if any have been made. Only those items in bolder print contain some information and can be activated.

The **pressing of the "ESC"** (escape) key will return you to previous screens.

2. **"F6=Family."** Pressing "F6" brings up the FAMILY GROUP RECORDS window and the choice of the person as a spouse or as a child with parents. Move the bar with the down or up arrow and make your choice with "Enter." After the family group records information appears, the windows for brief and detailed individual information are available for anyone on the record by moving the bar over their name and pressing "Enter." Also the **"F7=Pedigree"** function can be selected for anyone on the family group record.

To exit this part of the program press "F5=Index" which will return you to your list of names.

3. **"F7=Pedigree."** This function of the *Ancestral File* is one that is exciting and perhaps the most useful. The person you select becomes the first person on the pedigree and you WAIT with interest as the computer builds a five generation pedigree right before your eyes. Following the names of the five generations are arrows that indicate that additional generations follow that name. To extend a line move the bar over the arrow following their name with the up, down, left and right arrow keys and press "Enter." The windows for brief and detailed individual information, plus a window for children ("F11"), are also available for anyone on the pedigree record by moving the bar over their name and pressing "Enter." Also the **"F8=Descendancy"** function may be selected for anyone on the pedigree with the arrow

keys and by pressing "Enter." The preparation, printing, or downloading of a descendancy chart by the computer is very time consuming. Please remember, computer time is usually just a one hour slot and you will not be permitted to infringe on the next researcher's time. The "F8=Descendancy" function may also be chosen from the beginning list of names.

The pedigree on the screen provides only names; however, a printout through the use of "F2=Print/copy" includes their dates and places of birth, marriage, and death. From the PRINT/COPY window choose **"Print Pedigree Chart" and press "Enter."** The PRINT PEDIGREE CHART gives you several choices. One important one is to select a **6 generation CHART TYPE** if your pedigree indicates with an arrow at the end of a fifth generation person that additional generations are available. To choose a 6 generation printout, move the bar with the down arrow over **"6 Generations per page"** and press "Enter" and **"F12"** to print. Another window will appear with more selections and the ability to print family group records for each couple. Please choose **"Do NOT print family group records" and press "Enter"**, as it takes a great deal of time and costs a lot for all of the family group records, as you are charged for all printouts. The next window, PEDIGREE CHART NUMBER, permits you to number them as you wish. If in doubt and you don't care how they are numbered, type 1 in the "Chart Number:" bar and press "F12." While the printer is printing or the computer is compiling a file for downloading to a disk, you may proceed with your searching. If you want to print all of the family group records and have enough time and money to do so, then move the bar over either "Print family groups with LDS dates" or "Print family groups without LDS dates" and press "Enter." A screen with a list of the selected options will appear. Press either "Enter" if it is okay or "Esc" to cancel it if it is not okay. If you press "Esc" it will return you to the print selection menu again.

The **"F10=Go-back"** function permits you to return to names and the functions that have been used for those persons during your search and to reactivate those functions.

Researchers with computers and genealogical software that can receive GEDCOM data (Genealogical Data Communications, a computer

standard for transferring genealogical information) may download to
their preformated disks, in all sizes, any printable data from the
Ancestral File by following the prompts of "Create GEDCOM file of
ancestors. "

Ancestral File may also be used to edit, revise, change, and make
additions to itself. Inquire at a Family History Center or write the
Family History Library, 35 North West Temple Street, Salt Lake City,
UT 84150 (801) 240-2331 for the instructions, *FamilySearch:
Contributing Information to Ancestral File*" (3d ed., Salt Lake City:
The Church Jesus Christ of Latter-day Saints, 1992) and *FamilySearch:
Correcting Information in Ancestral File*" (Salt Lake City: Corporation
of the President of The Church Jesus Christ of Latter-day Saints, 1991).

FAMILY REGISTRY

The *Family Registry* is another source to check in your surveying
completed research. It was introduced in 1983 by the Family History
Department of the Church of Jesus Christ of Latter-day Saints for
researchers and representatives of family organizations as an aid to the
coordination of research. Thousands of people have registered their
research needs. The twenty-sixth edition, published in March 1992,
contains 336,341 registrations. Registration was not restricted to
members of the LDS Church; seventy-six percent of the registrants
were not members. The *Family Registry* is available on microfiche in
the Family History Library and its Centers in the United States and
Canada and in some genealogical libraries and genealogical departments
of public libraries.

When the *Family Registry* was introduced it was organized in two parts:
the "Registration Forms" and an "Index." Upon receipt, the
"Registration Forms" were given a number and then microfiched in
numerical order. The "Index" is arranged in alphabetical order, by
surnames (for the registration of family organizations) and by ancestors
(for individuals). Each index entry for individuals includes vital dates
(the year only); the country (including foreign countries) and state; sex;
researcher who submitted the information, and a registration number.

Chapter 4

Besides the above information, the "Registration Forms" usually contain the complete dates for vital events, the city and county where those events took place, the date the form was submitted, an alternate name and address in case the person who submitted the form was no longer available for contact, and additional notes that might be helpful in research. Registration forms received after March 20, 1985 and numbered after 96641 were not added to the "Registration Forms" part of the *Family Registry*. That part ends with microfiche sheet number 248 of microfiche collection number 6050001. The microfiche number for the index is 6050000. A list of the abbreviations used in the index appears in frames D 01 and E 01 of each microfiche.

Sample *Family Registry* Index Entry

NAMES SEX DATES/PLACES RELATIVES REG.NO. CONTACT
PERSON

WEEKS F B.1769?-USA/NC F.JABEZ WEEKS FR 13288
TAMAR D.1852 -USA/LA M.MARY RHODES   LURLINE
      M.1796   SP.DANIEL SANDERS   STANLEY
                            ROUTE 2 BOX 75
                            DIANA
                            TX 75640
                            USA
                            PH:214 968-6438

I. FAMILY HISTORY CENTER USERS:

The *FamilySearch*'s *Ancestral File* is available in most Family History Centers in the United States and Canada. If the *Ancestral File* on *FamilySearch* is available at a Family History Center near you, it is highly recommended that you search it before traveling to the Family History Library.

Other resources that help researchers get together are the *Family Registry*, *Computerized "Roots" Cellar*, and the *Genealogical Helper*, which contains the "Bureau of Missing Ancestors" column, Both the *Computerized "Roots" Cellar* and the *Genealogical Helper* are publications of the Everton Publishers, Inc.

II. LOCAL PUBLIC LIBRARY USERS:

Some public and genealogical libraries have acquired the *Family Registry* and *Computerized "Roots" Cellar*. Many of them also subscribe to the *Genealogical Helper*, of which the "Bureau of Missing Ancestors" column should be checked through the index to each copy of the magazine. You will probably have to wait until you are able to do research at the Family History Library in order to use the *Ancestral File* on *FamilySearch*.

III. HOME LIBRARY USERS:

A subscription to the *Genealogical Helper* may be useful. It is published by the Everton Publishers, Inc., P.O. Box 368, Logan, Utah 84321, (801) 752-6022. If you wish to check the *Family Registry* while at the Family History Library, copies are available on the main floor near the Information Desk. Make sure that you have a pedigree and the cards explained in chapter 1 in order to effectively use the *Ancestral File* on *FamilySearch*. It would also be helpful to read the *Genealogical Helper*'s regular feature, "Family History Library News."

ADDITIONAL READING:

All of the following are available at the Family History Library and its Centers:

FamilySearch: Using Ancestral File". 2d ed. Series AF, No. 2. Salt Lake City: Corporation of the President of The Church Jesus Christ of Latter-day Saints, 1990. 4 pages.

Chapter 4

"Ancestral File: Getting Started." 3d ed. Salt Lake City: The Church Jesus Christ of Latter-day Saints, 1992. 41 pages. In *"FamilySearch"* [manuals in binder].

FamilySearch: Correcting Information in Ancestral File". Series AF, No. 4. Salt Lake City: Corporation of the President of The Church Jesus Christ of Latter-day Saints, 1991. 4 pages.

FamilySearch: Contributing Information to Ancestral File". Salt Lake City: The Church Jesus Christ of Latter-day Saints, 1992. 4 pages.

SUMMARY:

The *Ancestral File* on *FamilySearch* is a very popular file and will probably grow at a rapid rate, as everyone is invited to submit their research to it. However, it does have some errors. The "Research interest" and "Family organizations" functions of the *Ancestral File* that appear on the "Sources" window are not yet operational. When they have been fully developed they may replace the *Family Registry*. Write the contributors to the *Ancestral File* and the registrants of the *Family Registry* who are researching the same ancestors. The *Ancestral File* is the largest single source for locating common ancestors. Through its use, many researchers have found other researchers and genealogists who are researching common lines. All researchers should consult it. Please remember to structure your computer time, which is usually limited to one hour, in order not to infringe on the reserved time of others.

"Just look at this pedigree [from the *Ancestral File*]!"

-- Excited researcher, Turlock Family History Center, 1992

Chapter 5

DOES YOUR FAMILY HAVE
A PRINTED HISTORY?

Another aspect of surveying completed research is determining if a family's research has already been published or is available as a manuscript family history. Hundreds of hours of research can be saved if a family history is found. Some family histories contain errors; nevertheless, they can still help answer puzzles about who and from where, even if researchers need to verify some of the data.

Family histories usually contain some information concerning the countries of origin. Most genealogical libraries in the United States include some family histories for families in foreign countries.

I. FAMILY HISTORY CENTER USERS:

Arrange your family surname cards, or computer lists prepared from instructions in chapter 1, in alphabetical order and consult the *Surname Catalog* of the *Family History Library Catalog* for each family. The *Surname Catalog* contains seven times as many references to allied or collateral lines as do the Library of Congress catalogs mentioned later in this chapter. The Family History Library has an estimated 41,000 family histories in book form alone. The Library also has additional family histories that are only available in the collection in microform. A study some time ago indicated that twenty-three percent of the Library's family history collection is not found in other collections.

This catalog is available also on the CD-ROM computer system, *FamilySearch*. The microfiche edition is available in all Family History Centers. *FamilySearch* is available in most Family History Centers, the Family History Library, and will be available in 1993 in the *FamilySearch* Center in the historic Hotel Utah building, South Temple and Main Streets. Both versions of the catalog are prepared and released at different dates. You should check the dates of each and use

the latest release or edition. The date for the microfiche is printed at
the top of each microfiche. The date for the catalog on *FamilySearch*
appears on the LIBRARY CATALOG MAIN MENU.

Sample
Microfiche
Family History Library Catalog: Surname Catalog Entry

COLE

```
                                    + ---------------- +
                                    :U.S. & CAN
King, Larry, 1909-                  :BOOK AREA
   Keith kinfolks : descendants of James    :929.273
   Keith, Sr., from 1720 to 1979 / by       :K269a
   Larry King. -- Hendersonville,           + ---------------- +
   Tenn. : King, c1979. -- [16],
   363 p. : ports.
```

James Keith (b. ca. 1720) immigrated from England to
   Virginia "...(brought) as an infant by relatives of
   a guardian." Many descendants moved westward.
Includes index.
Includes Alderman, Buckner, Cole, Hylton, King,
   Sutphin and related families.

Also on microfilm. Salt Lake City :   U.S. & CAN
   Filmed by the Genealogical Society of   FILM AREA
   Utah, 1986.   1321234
   on 1 microfilm reel ; 35 mm.   item 6.

Bibliographic 3"x5" cards should be prepared for the family histories
that you would like to consult at the Family History Library.
Bibliographic cards should contain the call number (also microform
number), author's full name, book title, place of publication, publisher,
date of publication, number of pages, and a note about whether or not
the book or microform has an index.

Does Your Family Have a Printed History?

Sample Family History Bibliographic Card

Alison Family

Morrison, Leonard Allison.
The history of the Alison or Allison
family in Europe and America. A.D. 1135-1893;
giving an account of the family in Scotland,
England, Ireland, Australia, Canada, and the
United States. Boston, Mass., 1893.
312 p. index. illus., ports.

U.S. & Can
Q area
929.273
AL48n

U.S. & Can
film area
1036444
item 12
FHLC CD-ROM 10/91

SURNAME CATALOG ON *FAMILYSEARCH*

If your Family History Center has *FamilySearch*, you may want to
search for family histories in it through the following computer choices
(selections), or ask a volunteer for help:

"Family History Library Catalog" from the FAMILYSEARCH
MAIN MENU.

"Surname Search" from the LIBRARY CATALOG MAIN MENU.

Press "Enter," type the surname of the family of interest, and press
"Enter."

In a few seconds the surnames and a few names of individuals with the
designated surname and variant spellings may appear on the screen, or
you may need to read down the screen or press the page down key
(PgDn) until you see a name of interest. If you find an individual of
interest, move the highlighted bar with the up or down arrow keys over
that name, and if only one record relates to that person press **"F8 = Full**

Display" for a full display of the book about whom or in which the individual appears. You will usually have to page down in order to read the entire record. If the record is of interest, please make the necessary bibliographic notes in order to obtain the work for use, or print the record by pressing **"F2 = Print."** Select **"Print the full list or record"** from the PRINT MENU by pressing **"Enter."** While the printer is printing you may proceed with your searching and queue up additional print commands. Researchers with computers may download to their preformated disks, in all sizes, any entries from the *Family History Library Catalog* by following the prompts of **"Copy data to disk."** Entries may then be transferred to most word-processing programs, but not to the *Personal Ancestral File.*

If two or more records are available for one person press **"F7 = Title/Notes"** and the system will display summaries of all of the records. Arrow down until you read all the records or select the one(s) you wish to display, then display it (them) using **"F8."**

After searching the individuals return to the top of the list of surnames by pressing **"F5 = Begin"** and then the **"Home"** key, which is usually on the right of the keyboard. The "Exact Match" entry usually cites a large number of records. The most efficient way to search a large collection of records is to limit the number of records displayed by pressing the **"F6" key which permits you to "Add Key-word,"** really two words or phrases. By typing in one or two of your related or collateral lines, the maternal lines on a pedigree (examples Keith and King), you can reduce that large file to a very small number, often one, maybe none. This type of collateral line search will often bring up a book that is about your family.

WARNING! If the "Exact Match" entry contains over four hundred records and you command the computer with the "F7" key to display summaries of all your search, you may overwork the computer. It will rebel with a big red window message stating that it can't take it, and it will drop your search and start itself up again as if the Family History Center just opened. Don't despair, you didn't hurt the computer, you just wasted your time.

Does Your Family Have a Printed History?

You can do a simple "Add Key-word" search by using the name of a city, county, state, region, country of origin, or residence to limit the number of records displayed. If you really want to search through several hundred records, it is faster to do it with the microfiche edition. You should read them on microfiche sometime.

II. Local Public Library Users:

Find out if your library has a copy of any of the following:

U.S. Library of Congress. *Genealogies in the Library of Congress: A Bibliography.* Edited by Marion J. Kaminkow. 2 vols. Baltimore: Magna Carta Book Co., 1972.
    FHL U.S. & CAN REF AREA 016.9291 K128g.

U.S. Library of Congress. *Genealogies in the Library of Congress: A Bibliography. Supplement, 1972-1976.* Baltimore: Magna Carta Book Co., 1977. FHL U.S. & CAN REF AREA 016.9291 K128g supp.

U.S. Library of Congress. *Genealogies in the Library of Congress: A Bibliography. Second Supplement, 1976-1986.* Baltimore: Magna Carta Book Co., 1987.
    FHL U.S. & CAN REF AREA 016.9291 K128g supp. 1987.

U.S. Library of Congress. *Genealogies Cataloged by the Library of Congress Since 1986: With a List of Established Forms of Family Names and a List of Genealogies Converted to Microfilm Since 1983.* Washington, D.C.: Library of Congress, 1992.

Complement to Genealogies in the Library of Congress Baltimore: Magna Carta Book Co., 1981.
    FHL U.S. & CAN REF AREA 016.9291 K128c.

These titles should be checked against your family surname cards or lists.

Chapter 5

Sample *Genealogies in the Library of Congress* Entry

15378 SHARP. Know your relatives: the Sharps, Gibbs, Graves, Efland, Albright, Loy, Miller, Snodderly, Tillman, and other related families. By Genevieve Elizabeth (Cummings) Peters. (Arlington? Va.) 1953. 169 p. 28 cm. 58-49595.

CS71.S53 1953

Sample *Complement to Genealogies* Entry

SHARP. Christian Sharp family genealogy. By Eli Sharp. Kansas City, Mo., 1952. 5 leaves. FW

(FW = This book is available at the Allen County Public Library, Fort Wayne, Indiana.)

These bibliographies are arranged by family surname. To use them simply look up surnames of interest. Check all of the names, dates, and places that are mentioned in each entry for each surname to see if an ancestor can be recognized, or a place where ancestors lived. The first two volumes of the *Genealogies in the Library of Congress* and the *Complement to Genealogies in the Library of Congress* have addenda that must also be checked. When reading the entries in these bibliographies, all the notes should be read as well; they may contain clues about who the principal ancestor was and in which part of the country an ancestor may have resided. If you know that the ancestor for whom you are looking was from New York and that the family moved west through Ohio, Nebraska, and Colorado to California, a family history about a family from Georgia is probably not yours.

Does Your Family Have a Printed History?

For any book that appears to be of interest, write down the author's full name, the title of the book, publisher, place and date of publication, number of pages, the Library of Congress call number (example: CS71 B213 1976).

Sample Family History Bibliographic Card

Sharp Family   CS71.S53 1953
  Know your relatives: the Sharps, Gibbs, Graves,
Efland, Albright, Loy, Miller, Snodderly, Tillman, and
other related families. By Genevieve Elizabeth
(Cummings) Peters. Arlington, Va., 1953. 169 p.

Your public library may purchase the microfilm edition of the *Family History Library Catalog: Surname Catalog.*

While at the Family History Library take the family surname cards or lists and the bibliographic cards prepared from the above catalogs and check them against the *Family History Library Catalog: Surname Catalog.* Prepare additional bibliographic cards for family histories of interest and add FHL book or microfilm numbers to any books listed on bibliographic cards and prepared from the Library of Congress Catalogs.

III. HOME LIBRARY USERS:

You may write to the Family History Library, 35 North West Temple Street, Salt Lake City, Utah 84150, and ask them to photocopy portions of the *Family History Library Catalog: Surname Catalog.* There is a small fee for this service. You may also purchase the microfiche edition of it for use at your nearest library that has a microfiche reader.

Chapter 5

ADDITIONAL READING:

Parker, J. Carlyle. "Finding Family Histories," chapter 8, pages 105-117. In *Library Service for Genealogists.* Gale Genealogy and Local History Series, vol. 15. Detroit: Gale Research Co., 1981, op. 2d edition in progress by Marietta Publishing Co.
   FHL U.S. & CAN REF AREA 026.9291 P226L.

SUMMARY:

Checking the *Surname Catalog* of the *Family History Library Catalog* for a family history before you go to Salt Lake City for research is very important. The *Surname Catalog* will help you locate the most important books and microfilm to read in the Library and save you from a long catalog search while you're there.

If the *Family History Library Catalog* is not readily available to you, check the *Genealogies in the Library of Congress: A Bibliography,* its supplements, *Genealogies Cataloged by the Library of Congress Since 1986: With a List of Established Forms of Family Names and a List of Genealogies Converted to Microfilm Since 1983,* and the *Complement to Genealogies in the Library of Congress.* After you have used either the *Family History Library Catalog: Surname Catalog* or the Library of Congress bibliographies, you should check the other.

"Whew! I don't know which is harder, this [research] or housework."

-- Female researcher overheard in the Family History
Library bookstacks, 1992

Chapter 6

FAMILY HISTORY LIBRARY CATALOG

Use of the *Family History Library Catalog* is imperative because of the Library's vast collections of books and records on microfilm and microfiche. If you try browsing your way through the book collection you will waste hours of research time. Browsing through microforms is impossible because there are very few library-generated titles on the microfilm boxes, and all microforms are arranged in numerical order and not arranged in subject or geographical order.

The *Family History Library Catalog* is available in all Family History Centers. A few public and genealogical libraries have also purchased the *Family History Library Catalog*. However, you may have to wait until you arrive at the Family History Library.

The *Family History Library Catalog* is on microfiche and on *FamilySearch* and is divided into four sections: *Locality Catalog*, *Surname Catalog* (already explained in chapter 5), *Subject Catalog*, and *Author/Title Catalog*. The later two catalogs are currently (1992) not on *FamilySearch*. Checking the *Family History Library Catalog: Locality Catalog* can be done simply by utilizing the 3"x5" geographical cards or computer lists that were discussed in chapter 1.

Locality Catalog on microfiche

Look in the *Family History Library Catalog: Locality Catalog* for vital records of the geographical areas and periods of time that relate to your ancestors of interest. Vital records are the most important resource for genealogical research. They include the registration of births, marriages, deaths, and divorces, as well as U.S. mortality census schedules (June 1, 1849 - May 31, 1850; June 1, 1859 - May 31, 1860; June 1, 1869 - May 31, 1870; June 1, 1879 - May 31, 1880) and mortuary records. Microfilmed vital records are the cheapest, often the fastest, and in many cases the easiest way to obtain this information about ancestors. The Library has large collections of civil and church vital records from the sixteenth through nineteenth centuries. Records in the library's largest collections are from the United States, Canada, Mexico, Philippines and most countries of western Europe (including the Azores of Portugal), and Poland.

However, the records at the Family History Library that are available for public use usually protect the current rights of privacy. Therefore, available microfilm often does not include twentieth century records that might contain information about living persons.

The subject headings for vital records used in the *Locality Catalog* of the *Family History Library Catalog* are like these examples:

OHIO, ROSS - VITAL RECORDS
OHIO, ROSS, CHILLICOTHE - VITAL RECORDS.

Sample
Family History Library Catalog: Locality Catalog
Entry on Microfiche

OHIO, ROSS - VITAL RECORDS

```
                                    +-------------+
                                    :U.S. & CAN
Ohio.  Probate Court (Ross County).  :FILM AREA
    Birth records, 1867-1908; index to    +-------------+
    birth records, 1867-1908. -- Salt Lake
    City : Filmed by the Genealogical Society
    of Utah, 1962. -- 3 microfilm reels ; 35 mm.
```

Microfilm of original records in the Ross
County courthouse, Chillicothe, Ohio.
Records are not in order by date.
Includes indexes at the beginning of each
volume.

Index, v. 1-2   1867-1908 ------------- 0281655
Births, v. 1-3   1867-1889 ------------- 0281656
Births, v. 4-5   1889-1908 ------------- 0281657

As you identify materials of interest you should make bibliographic cards for them. Also make note of the date of the *Family History Library Catalog* that you have used, since the catalog is updated periodically. This date is in the caption at the top of each microfiche and can be read without a microfiche reading machine. This may help resolve problems that you might encounter while using the Family History Library due to a change in the catalog, such as a changed call number. The microfiche and *FamilySearch* versions of the catalog are prepared and released at different dates. You should check the dates of each and use the latest release or edition. The date for the catalog on *FamilySearch* appears on the LIBRARY CATALOG MAIN MENU.

Sample Bibliographic Card

Ohio, Ross Co.	U.S. & Can
Births	film area
Index, v. 1-2 1867-1908	0281655
Births, v. 1-3 1867-1889	0281656
Births, v. 4-5 1889-1908	0281657

FHLC CD-ROM 10/91

Both the county and city subdivisions of a state should be searched for vital records. In addition, for some states and countries it may be necessary to look under the state or country name because the records may have been collected at the state or country level.

If government vital records are not listed in the *Family History Library Catalog: Locality Catalog* or when they fail to provide needed information, researchers should try to determine the religion of their ancestors and turn to church records for vital data and other information collected, recorded, and preserved by churches. Because church records have not been as widely microfilmed as civil records, it is not as easy to locate them as it is civil or government records, but it is not an impossible task.

The subject headings for searching church records in the *Family History Library Catalog: Locality Catalog* are like these examples:

OHIO, ROSS - CHURCH RECORDS
OHIO, ROSS, CHILLICOTHE - CHURCH RECORDS

Besides the church records that substitute for vital records (baptisms, christenings, marriages and their banns, and church burials) the locality subject heading subdivision "CHURCH RECORDS" includes other miscellaneous records, such as church membership lists and church censuses that may also be helpful in genealogical research.

Researchers can turn to cemetery records when government and church records are not available at the Family History Library, or, if available, do not include your people. Many cemetery records have been collected and published by various genealogical and hereditary societies and by individuals. Often these cemetery records are based on headstone inscriptions. Occasionally, they are based on the records of the cemetery's sexton.

The sexton's records are the better of the two, as there are many cemetery burial plots not marked with headstones. However, headstone inscriptions may contain additional information, including relationships, that may not be provided in the sexton's records. The following are the subject headings under which cemetery records may be found in the *Family History Library Catalog: Locality Catalog*:

OHIO, ROSS - CEMETERIES
OHIO, ROSS, CHILLICOTHE - CEMETERIES

Other useful records are wills and probates. You should bear in mind that wills and probates usually do not contain the names of deceased, disowned, or lost children. They are cataloged in the *Family History Library Catalog: Locality Catalog* under the following subject headings:

OHIO, ROSS - PROBATE RECORDS
OHIO, ROSS - PROBATE RECORDS - INDEXES

Land records often include the sale of property from parent to child and may provide information concerning relationships. Land records subject headings in the *Family History Library Catalog: Locality Catalog* are:

OHIO, ROSS - LAND AND PROPERTY
OHIO, ROSS - LAND AND PROPERTY - INDEXES

The Library also has the following additional sources that supplement vital records: adoption records, Bible records, census schedules, guardianships, retroactive military pension applications, naturalization records, obituaries and necrologies, orphan records, and passenger lists. The following list provides the *Family History Library Catalog: Locality Catalog* subject headings for these records:

Subject or Record Type	Locality Subject Heading Subdivision
Adoptions	COURT RECORDS
	GUARDIAN AND WARD RECORDS
Census schedules	CENSUS
Family Bibles	BIBLE RECORDS
Guardianships	GUARDIAN AND WARD
Military retroactive pension applications	MILITARY RECORDS - PENSIONS
Naturalization records	NATURALIZATION AND CITIZENSHIP
Necrologies	OBITUARIES
Obituaries	OBITUARIES
Orphan records	ORPHANS AND ORPHANAGES
Passenger lists	EMIGRATION AND IMMIGRATION

Chapter 6

It is efficient use of the *Catalog* to read it backwards, starting with the "Vital Records" of city, county, or state and moving towards the front of the locality catalog through "Probate Records," "Land Records," "Church Records," "Census Records," and "Biography." Following this backwards reading method, the records are arranged generally in order of importance.

FAMILYSEARCH

If your Family History Center has *FamilySearch*, you may want to search the *Family History Library Catalog* for vital records, probate records, or land records by the names of your counties, looking at the "Locality Search." Please ask a volunteer for help if you have any problems using any of the computer programs on *FamilySearch*. To get to "Locality Search" choose (select) in the following order:

"Family History Library Catalog" from the FAMILYSEARCH MAIN MENU by placing the bar over the "Family History Library Catalog" line with the down arrow and by **pressing "Enter."**

Then choose **"Locality Search"** from the LIBRARY CATALOG MAIN MENU by **pressing "Enter."**

If you wish to limit your search to a town or parish, then choose **"Town and parish records"** from the LOCALITY REQUEST screen by **pressing "Enter."**

However, for research in the United States, except for the New England states and a very few independent cities, such as Richmond, Virginia, you should skip town records, as such a search is too limiting. Search first for research materials at the county subject subdivision of the catalog, then the town or city, and finally at the state subject subdivision.

Instead, arrow down so that the bar is over **"County or non-Canadian province records" and press "Enter,"** and type in the name of the county of interest, and **press "Enter."**

If you wish to limit your search to vital records, type that into the barred area to the right of **"Topic:"** and press **"Enter."**

However, **you should leave the "Topic:" area blank and simply press "Enter."** A search of just one topic may be too limiting, perhaps misleading, and not as thorough as a search of "ALL" topics.

At the **"Country/State:"** bar type in the state of the United States, province of Canada, or name of foreign country.

In all of the above processes type out full place names, not abbreviations.

The screen will normally display a long list of topics; page and arrow down to the last and usually most useful topic, "Vital records." From "Vital records" use the following process to read back to the top of the list the records that may be of interest to you:

With the bar over **"Vital records"** press **"F7 = Author/Title"** for topics with two or more records or **"F8 = Full Display"** for topics with only one record.

When searching two or more records on the "F7 = Author/Title" screen, arrow down as you read each record and with the bar over the entry you wish to choose to read press "F8 = Full Display." Make the necessary notes or print the record by pressing **"F2 = Print."** Select "Print the full list or record" from the PRINT MENU by pressing "Enter." While the printer is printing you may proceed with your searching and queue up additional print commands. Researchers with computers may download to their preformated disks, in all sizes, any entries from the *Family History Library Catalog* by following the prompts of **"Copy data to disk."** Entries may then be transferred to most word-processing programs, but not to the *Personal Ancestral File.*

To return to the list of topics, press "F6 = Topic(s)," move the bar with the up arrow and press "Enter" at your next record(s) of choice. It is faster to search through multiple records on the microfiche edition of the *Family History Library Catalog.*

Chapter 6

Two vital record files are also available on *FamilySearch*. The *Military Index* contains the death records of United States military service persons who died or were declared dead in the Korean (1950 to 1957) and Vietnam (1957-1975) conflicts. It contains birth and death dates, race, residence at the time of enlistment, rank, branch of service and number, and place of death. For casualties of the Vietnam conflict, their religious affiliation and marital status were added. A one-page publication available at Family History Centers and the Family History Library that explains the index is *FamilySearch: Military Index* (Series FS, No.2, Salt Lake City: Corporation of the President of The Church Jesus Christ of Latter-day Saints, 1991).

The second file is the *Social Security Death Index*, which contains brief information on 39.5 million deceased persons, 1937-1988, best coverage of which is from 1962-1988. It provides for, but does not always give, birth and death dates, the state in which application was made, the last place of residence, and/or where a death benefit was sent.

Women's married names, instead of their maiden names, are used for searching the *Social Security Death Index*. The application card of those listed may be obtained by sending the ancestor's Social Security number with a check or money order payable to the Social Security Administration for $7.00 to the Freedom of Information Officer, 4-H-8 Annex Building, 6401 Security Blvd., Baltimore, MD 21235.

The data on these files can be limited geographically by state by pressing the "F10=Filter" key after having typed in the "Surname" or "Birth year." Both files may be printed or downloaded to computer disks. These indexes are a United States government document and may be available in some public and university libraries. The Family History Centers and the Family History Library also have a four page pamphlet, *Social Security Death Index* (Series FS, No. 3, Salt Lake City: Corporation of the President of The Church of Jesus Christ of Latter-day Saints, 1990).

There may be other works that have been or will be brought to your attention in your research that may not be easily found through the use of the *Locality Catalog* of the *Family History Library Catalog*. The

Author/Title Catalog of the *Family History Library Catalog* may be used if an author or title is known, or the *Surname Catalog* of the *Family History Library Catalog* if only a family name is known. The *Author/Title Catalog* is not available on *FamilySearch*.

The *Subject Catalog* of the *Family History Library Catalog* contains, in part, the following selected list of subjects that may be of interest to some researchers:

> COLLEGE, used as the second word following the name of the college; example: ST. MARY'S COLLEGE (ST. MARYS, KANSAS). A useful subdivision of this type of entry is BIOGRAPHY, where you would find biographical sketches of graduates and those who served in various wars.
>
> CONFEDERATE STATES OF AMERICA - MILITARY RECORDS - CIVIL WAR, 1861-1865.
>
> DICTIONARIES - ENGLISH, used as the subject heading subdivision for English language dictionaries of another language; example: FINNISH LANGUAGE - DICTIONARIES - ENGLISH.
>
> GENEALOGY, used for general genealogical how-to-do-it books.
>
> INDIANS, used as the second word following a tribal name; example: CAYUGA INDIANS.
>
> INDIANS OF NORTH AMERICA - NEBRASKA and nearly all of the other states of the union.
>
> INDIANS OF NORTH AMERICA - UNITED STATES
> United States. Bureau of Indian Affairs.
> Indian census rolls, 1885-1940. 692 reels.
>
> Minorities; examples: ACADIANS - QUEBEC - GENEALOGY.
>
> > AFRO-AMERICANS - GENEALOGY - VIRGINIA.
> > AMERICAN LOYALISTS - NEW JERSEY.
>
> NEW ENGLAND - GENEALOGY.
>
> Religions' general records, histories, etc.; examples:
> > MORMONS - GENEALOGY - SOURCES.
> > QUAKERS - GENEALOGY.
> > QUAKERS - UNITED STATES.
> > WALDENSES - ITALY.
>
> SOUTHERN STATES - GENEALOGY.

> UNIVERSITY - STUDENTS, used as the second word following the name of the university and subdivided by STUDENTS; example: ACADIA UNIVERSITY - STUDENTS. This heading usually covers works containing biographical sketches of graduates.

The *Subject Catalog* is not presently available on *FamilySearch*.

I. FAMILY HISTORY CENTER USERS:

You can save a great deal of time at the Family History Library if you consult the *Family History Library Catalog* and prepare bibliographic cards or computer lists for the materials you wish to consult before your trip to the Library. The *Family History Library Catalog* is available in all Family History Centers.

II. LOCAL PUBLIC LIBRARY USERS:

A few public and genealogical libraries have purchased the *Family History Library Catalog*. However, you may have to wait until you arrive at the Family History Library before you will have access to it, or follow the directions below in section III.

III. HOME LIBRARY USERS:

You may write to the Family History Library, 35 North West Temple, Salt Lake City, Utah 84150, and ask them to photocopy portions of the *Family History Library Catalog*. The microfiche edition of the catalog may also be purchased from the Library in total or in part by individuals for non-commercial use. The Family History Library offers classes on how to use the *Family History Library Catalog*.

Additional Viewing and Reading:

Family History Library. *How to Use the Family History Library Catalog*. Salt Lake City: Church of Jesus Christ of Latter-day Saints, 1987.
A 24-minute videocassette, available at the Family History Library and most Family History Centers.

FamilySearch: Family History Library Catalog (on compact disc) Getting Started. 3d ed. Series FHLCAT, No. 2. Salt Lake City: The Church Jesus Christ of Latter-day Saints, 1992. 4 pages.

"FamilySearch: Family History Library Catalog (on compact disc) Getting Started." 2d ed. Salt Lake City: Corporation of the President of The Church Jesus Christ of Latter-day Saints, 1990. 22 pages. In *"FamilySearch"* [manuals in binder].

"FamilySearch: *Social Security Death Index* (on compact disc) Getting Started." 2d ed. Salt Lake City: Corporation of the President of The Church Jesus Christ of Latter-day Saints, 1990. 13 pages. In *"FamilySearch"* [manuals in binder].

Additional information about vital records may be found in chapter 10, pages 151-79 of Val D. Greenwood's *The Researcher's Guide to American Genealogy* (2d ed., Baltimore: Genealogical Publishing Co., 1990, FHL U.S. & CAN REF AREA 973 D27g 1990). Greenwood covers church records in chapter 20, pages 423-63; cemetery records in chapter 24, pages 545-55; probate records in chapters 13-15 and 18, pages 255-320 and 379-96; and land records in chapters 16-18, pages 321-96.

SUMMARY:

Consulting the *Family History Library Catalog, Locality Catalog* before you go to Salt Lake City for research is perhaps the most important thing that you can do to save time while in Salt Lake City. It should be checked particularly for vital records for all places where ancestors lived, as well as supplemental vital records.

CENSUS TAKER

Martha Porter and children with U.S. census taker, Orderville, Utah 1910.
Photograph by F. Alvin Porter, 1878-1976.

Chapter 7

ARE YOUR ANCESTORS IN THE
U.S. FEDERAL CENSUS SCHEDULES?

If any one of your ancestors lived in the United States during the years 1790, 1800, 1810, 1820, 1830, 1840, 1850, 1860, 1870, 1880, 1900, 1910, or 1920, he or she probably can be found in the federal census schedules. The census schedules from 1850 on are the most useful, as they include the names of all members of households at the time of the census and increase in the amount of genealogical information with each succeeding census. The earlier census schedules give only the names of the heads of households and the age and sex of the members of the households. All of the microfilm copies of the U.S. federal census schedules are available at the Family History Library; the National Archives, Washington, D.C.; and its twelve regional archives.

The Family History Library also has some state census schedules that were taken in the mid-census years; for example, Kansas 1855, 1865, 1875, and 1885. There are also census schedules available at the Family History Library for Canada, England, Scotland, and Wales (1841-1891); and Denmark (1787-1911), Iceland (1762-1901), and Norway (1664-1900). Among the church records for Sweden are clerical surveys, which can be used as a substitute for census records.

There are many published state-wide indexes for the United States federal census schedules for the years 1790 through 1850. Some for more recent years have also been published, and many are currently in preparation for 1860 and 1870 and a few for Canada and England. A bibliography of hundreds of U.S. federal census schedule state-wide indexes is included in chapter 12, pages 139-89, "Census Schedules," in *Library Service for Genealogists* by J. Carlyle Parker (Gale Genealogy and Local History Series, vol. 15, Detroit: Gale Research Co, 1981, op, FHL U.S. & CAN REF AREA 026.9291 P226L; 2d edition in progress by Marietta Publishing Co.).

Chapter 7

At some point you will need to use the 1880, 1900, 1910, or 1920 Soundex and Miracode card indexes to the U.S. federal census schedules. The 1880 index includes only families with children age 10 and under. All families are indexed in the 1900 and 1920 census schedules. Index cards of the Soundex and Miracode were created only for the names of the heads of households and for persons residing in the same household with surnames different than the head of the household.

However, the Soundex and/or Miracodes for the 1910 schedules are only available for the following twenty-one states:

Alabama	Kentucky	Oklahoma
Arkansas	Louisiana	Pennsylvania
California	Michigan	South Carolina
Florida	Mississippi	Tennessee
Georgia	Missouri	Texas
Illinois	North Carolina	Virginia
Kansas	Ohio	West Virginia

Before you use a Soundex or Miracode you need to determine the soundex codes for all of your surnames of research interest and add the number to your 3"x5" cards or computer lists.

Soundex Code on the *Personal Ancestral File* and *FamilySearch*

A part of the computer program, *Personal Ancestral File* (*PAF*), mentioned elsewhere in this guide, completes this task with record speed. The *PAF* is also available at Family History Centers with the computer CD-ROM *FamilySearch*. The soundex codes may be found through the following choices (selections) by pressing:

"1" for **Family Records** from the ACCESS MENU. After this choice the program will ask you to "Put Your Family Record data disk in drive A." You may insert a blank formatted disk.

"9" for **Facts and Fun** from the MAIN MENU.

Are Your Ancestors in the Census?

"2" for SOUNDEX from the FACTS AND FUN MENU.

Type in surname of interest and press return and soundex code will appear on the screen, example: S563.

The program will then report "No Match Found." Press "Enter" which will return you to the FACTS AND FUN MENU.

Press "2" again for SOUNDEX (type in another surname).

To end the search choose the following:

"0" for Return to Main Menu from the FACTS AND FUN MENU.

"0" for Return to System from the MAIN MENU.

"Enter" at Backup Reminder!

"O" for Return to System from the ACCESS MENU

Don't forget to remove your disk.

Another resource for determining soundex codes is Bradley W. Steuart's *The Soundex Reference Guide: Soundex Codes to Over 125,000 Surnames* (Bountiful, Utah: Precision Indexing, 1990, FHL U.S. & CAN REF AREA 973 D27so).

The accuracy of both of the above are superior to the use of the standard instructions which follow, taken from the copyright-free U.S. federal census catalogs listed in part II, "Local Public Library Users," of this chapter:

Guide to the Soundex System

The Soundex filing system, alphabetic for the first letter of surname and numeric thereunder as indicated by divider cards, keeps together names of the same and similar sounds but of variant spellings.

Chapter 7

The Bureau of the Census created and filmed Soundex index cards for the entire 1920 census. The Soundex is a coded surname (last name) index based on the way a surname sounds rather than how it is spelled. Surnames that sound the same but are spelled differently, like SMITH and SMYTH, have the same code and are filed together. The Soundex coding system was developed to find a surname even though it may have been recorded under various spellings. The National Archives has assigned a separate microfilm publication for each state and territory.

The Bureau of the Census used two separate Soundex cards, the "family card" and the "individual card." Both types of cards are arranged numerically by the Soundex code and then alphabetically by the first name of the head of the household on the family cards and the first name of the individual on the individual cards.

Every Soundex code consists of a letter and three numbers, such as S-650. The letter is always the first letter of the surname, whether it is a vowel or a consonant. Disregard the remaining vowels and W, Y, and H and assign numbers to the next three consonants of the surname according to the Soundex coding guide. If there are not three consonants following the initial letter, use zeros to fill out the three-digit code.

Most surnames can be coded using the Soundex coding guide. Names with prefixes, double letters, or letters side by side that have the same number of the Soundex coding system are described below.

To search for a particular name, you must first work out the code number for the surname of the individual. No number is assigned to the first letter of the surname. If the name is Kuhne, for example, the index card will be in the "K" segment of the index. The code number for Kuhne, worked out according to the system below, is 500.

Soundex Coding Guide

The number   Represents the letters
  1   b, p, f, v
  2   c, s, k, g, j, q, x, z
  3   d, t
  4   l
  5   m, n
  6   r

The letters a, e, i, o, u, y, w, and h are not
 coded.
The first letter of a surname is not coded.
Every Soundex number must be a 3-digit number.
 A name yielding no code numbers, as Lee, would thus
 be L000; one yielding only one code number would
  have two zeros added, as Kuhne, coded as K500; and
  one yielding two code numbers would have one zero
  added, as Ebell, coded as E140. Not more than
  three digits are used, so Ebelson would be coded as
  E142, not E1425.

Names with Double Letters

When two key letters or equivalents appear together,
 or one key letter immediately follows or precedes
 an equivalent, the two are coded as one letter, by
 a single number, as follows: Ke_lly_, coded as K400;
 Buer_ck_, coded as B620; _Ll_oyd, coded as L300; and
 S_ch_aefer, coded as S160.

If several surnames have the same code, the cards for them
are arranged alphabetically by given name. There are
divider cards showing most code numbers, but not all. For
instance, one divider may be numbered 350 and the next
one 400. Between the two divider cards there may be
names coded 353, 350, 360, 364, 365, and 355, but instead
of being in numerical order they are inter-filed
alphabetically by given name.

Chapter 7

Names with Prefixes

If the surname has a prefix, such as "van," "Von," "de," "le," "Di," "D'," "dela," or "du" code it both with and without the prefix because it might be listed under either code. The surname vanDevanter, for example, could be V-531 or D-153. Mc and Mac are not considered prefixes.

Names With Letters Side by Side That Have The Same Number on the Soundex Coding Guide

A surname may have different letters that are side by side and have the same number on the Soundex coding guide; for example, PF in Pfister (1 is the number for both P and F); CKS in Jackson (2 is the number for C. K. and S). These letters should be treated as one letter. Thus in the name Pfister, F should be crossed out; in the name Jackson, K and S should be crossed out.

The following names are examples of Soundex coding and are given only as illustrations.

Name	Letters Coded	Code No.
Allricht	l, r, c	A 462
Eberhard	b, r, r	E 166
Engebrethson	n, g, b	E 521
Heimbach	m, b, c	H 512
Hanselmann	n, s, l	H 524
Henzelmann	n, z, l	H 524
Hildebrand	l, d, b	H 431
Kavanagh	v, n, g	K 152
Lind, Van	n, d	L 530
Lukaschowsky	k, s, s	L 222
McDonnell	c, d, n	M 235
McGee	c	M 200
O'Brien	b, r, n	O 165
Opnian	p, n, n	O 155

Oppenheimer	p, n, m	O 155
Riedemanas	d, m, n	R 355
Zita	t	Z 300
Zitzmeinn	t, z, m	Z 325

Native Americans, Orientals, and Religious Nuns

Researchers using the Soundex system to locate religious nuns or persons with American Indian or oriental names should be aware of the way such names were coded. Variations in coding differed from the normal coding system.

Phonetically spelled oriental and Indian names were sometimes coded as if one continuous name, or, if a distinguishable surname was given, the names were coded in the normal manner. For example, the American Indian name Shinka-Wa-Sa may have been coded as "Shinka" (S-520) or "Sa" (S-000). Researchers should investigate the various possibilities of coding such names.

Religious nun names were coded as if "Sister" were the surname, and they appear in the State's Soundex/Miracode under the code "S-236." Within the State's Soundex/Miracode code S-236, the names are not necessarily in alphabetical order.

Sample 1910 MIRACODE Entry

OKLAHOMA	OKLAHOMA CITY		049 0218 0317	
J162 JEFFERSON	ALLEN	H	M 32 TEXAS	OKLA
	MARY	W	30	TEXAS
GRAHAM	HENRIETTA	SD	15	TEXAS
DAVIS	SAMMIE	SS	11	TEXAS

Chapter 7

J162 is the Miracode code for the surname Jefferson; 049 is the volume number, not necessary to note; 0218 is the enumeration district; 0317 is the number of the family in order of visitation. Both of the latter numbers should be noted in order to find the family in the census schedule. Oklahoma is the county. The state is not recorded on each card.

The 1880, 1900, and 1920 Soundex cards are formatted and contain nearly the same information and are self-explanatory. Notes made from the Soundex should also include the county, city, the enumeration district number, and the sheet number and line number. These numbers are necessary to locate your ancestor on the census schedule for the county of residence. The line number is not provided on the 1910 Soundex cards.

After the Soundex or Miracode has been used, it is important that the census schedules be checked to determine if any errors were made in the Soundex or Miracode transcription and for additional information contained in the schedules.

I. Family History Center Users:

It is not necessary to look up the microfilm numbers for the census schedules and soundexes for the United States that you will use at the Family History Library as they are arranged in their cabinets by census year and state; and boxes are labeled just like the catalogs listed in part II, "Local Public Library Users," of this chapter. The census schedules for Canada are also arranged by year and province.

It is important to pay attention to the following note that appears on some reel box labels:

LISTINGS CONTINUED
ON THE SIDE OF BOX -->

However, if census schedules are ordered for use in a Family History Center, their microfilm numbers will have to be ascertained.

Are Your Ancestors in the Census?

The fastest way to determine the Family History Library's microfilm numbers for the federal census schedules is to consult the binders at a Family History Center labeled: U.S. CENSUS, 1790-1880; U.S. CENSUS, 1900; U.S. CENSUS, 1910; and U.S. CENSUS, 1920. These microfilm numbers are also included in the *Family History Library Catalog: Locality Catalog* on microfiche and *FamilySearch* under the subject heading "United States - Census - (year)." State census schedule microfilm numbers are listed in the *Family History Library Catalog: Locality Catalog* under the name of the state, subdivided by "Census - (year)."

Most of the older Family History Centers have the *AIS* (Accelerated Indexing Systems) consolidated indexes on microfiche for the 1790 through 1850 federal census schedules, including some earlier and later census schedules. It may be useful to check these indexes before going to the Family History Library to find the exact county and leaf number (which consists of the front and back of one leaf, or the equivalent of two pages) where your ancestors are listed.

The *Family History Library Catalog: Locality Catalog* on microfiche and *FamilySearch* also have the microfilm numbers for the census schedules of some foreign countries under the subject heading "(name of country) - Census - (year)."

As your research with the census progresses you may find that you must learn something about original counties and their boundaries. Suppose you are researching for ancestors in a particular county and find that that county is not listed in the federal census schedule catalog for 1870, or the community in which they lived is not in its present county or the county in which they were reported to have lived. Then you need to know what county in 1870 included the place where your ancestor was living. The following work may be able to help you solve your problem,

Thorndale, William, and Dollarhide, William. *Map Guide to the U.S. Federal Censuses, 1790-1920.* Baltimore: Genealogical Publishing Co., 1987. FHL U.S. & CAN REF AREA 973 X2th.
Shows 400 U.S. county boundary maps for the census decades from 1790 to 1920 superimposed on modern county boundaries.

Chapter 7

II. LOCAL PUBLIC LIBRARY USERS:

Some local public libraries will have copies of the National Archives, *Catalog of Federal Census Schedules*. There is no way to match the reel numbers in these catalogs with the microfilm numbers in the Family History Library. However, you can get an idea of what is available. Some of the larger public libraries, the National Archives, and its regional archives have some published copies of state-wide indexes to the federal census schedules which should be checked for ancestors in appropriate volumes.

The catalogs for the federal census schedules are as follows:

U.S. National Archives. *Federal Population Censuses 1790-1890: A Catalog of Microfilm Copies of the Schedules*. Publication 71-3. Washington, D.C.: Gov't. Print. Off., 1971-   GS4.2:P31/2/790-890.

U.S. National Archives. *1900 Federal Population Census: A Catalog of Microfilm Copies of the Schedules*. Washington, D.C.: Gov't. Print. Off., 1979.

U.S. National Archives and Records Service. *The 1910 Federal Population Census: A Catalog of Microfilm Copies of the Schedules*. Washington, D.C.: National Archives Trust Fund Board, 1982.

U.S. National Archives and Records Service. *The 1920 Federal Population Census: A Catalog of Microfilm Copies of the Schedules*. Washington, D.C.: National Archives Trust Fund Board, 1991.

Many libraries are able to obtain microfilm copies of the U.S. federal census schedules through interlibrary loan from their state libraries or through the rental services of the National Archives Microfilm Rental Program, P.O. Box 30, Annapolis Junction, MD 20701-0030, (301) 604-3699 or the American Genealogical Lending Library, P.O. Box 244, Bountiful, Utah 84011, (801) 298-5358 (800 657-9442), FAX (801) 298-5468.

III. HOME LIBRARY USERS:

You could purchase the above National Archives catalogs. However, the author would not recommend it. Just wait until you can go to either the Family History Center or a public library and use the above catalogs, or go to the National Archives in Washington, D.C. or to one of its twelve regional archives in Anchorage, East Point (near Atlanta), Waltham (near Boston), Chicago, Denver, Fort Worth, Kansas City, Laguna Niguel (near Los Angeles), Bayonne, N.J. (near New York City), Philadelphia, San Bruno (near San Francisco), or Seattle.

If you can't wait to read a federal census schedule and do not have access to a Family History Center, and if you cannot obtain them through the services of your public library, you can join either the National Archives Microfilm Rental Program, P.O. Box 30, Annapolis Junction, MD 20701-0030, (301) 604-3699 or the American Genealogical Lending Library, P.O. Box 244, Bountiful, Utah 84011, (801) 298-5358 (800 657-9442), FAX (801) 298-5468. The American Genealogical Lending Library also has some state census schedules.

Additional Viewing and Reading:

Genealogical Department. *How to Use the U.S. Census*. Salt Lake City: Church of Jesus Christ of Latter-day Saints, 1985.
   A 12-minute videocassette, available at the Family History Library and most Family History Centers.

U.S. National Archives and Records Service. "Census Records," chapter 1, pages 9-38. In *Guide to Genealogical Research in the National Archives*. Washington, D.C.: National Archives Trust Fund Board, 1983. FHL U.S. & CAN REF AREA 973 A3usn. FHL U.S. & CAN FICHE AREA & FHCs 6051414 (4 microfiche).

Parker, J. Carlyle. *City, County, Town, and Township Index to the 1850 Federal Census Schedules*. Gale Genealogy and Local History Series, Vol. 6. Detroit: Gale Research Co., 1979, op.
   FHL U.S. & CAN REF AREA 973 X22p.
   Microfiche. Turlock, Calif.: Marietta Publishing Co., 1990.

Chapter 7

The cities, towns, and townships in the 1850 schedules are not in alphabetical order in each county. This index has them in alphabetical order for the entire nation and provides the page numbers for the exact location of communities and townships on the microfilm of the census schedules, as well as the Family History Library and National Archives microfilm numbers.

Smith, Leonard H., Jr. *U.S. Census Key: 1850, 1860, 1870.*
Bountiful, Utah: American Genealogical Lending Library, 1986.
   FHL U.S. & CAN REF AREA 973 X2s 1850-1870.
   For counties that have two or more reels of microfilm this work lists the townships in the order in which they appear in the schedules.

Family History Library. *A Key to the 1880 United States Federal Census.* 2d rev. and corr. Bowie Md.: Heritage Books, 1986.
Bountiful, Utah: American Genealogical Lending Library, 199?
   FHL U.S. & CAN REF AREA 973 X2ch.
   Lists the first and last enumeration district and all district numbers on each microfilm reel, as well as the National Archives and Family History Library microfilm numbers.

SUMMARY:

Your American ancestors are probably recorded in some census schedules. The Family History Library has U.S. federal census schedules, as well as some state census schedules. It also has census schedules of many other countries. Because of the usefulness of census schedules, particularly those from 1850 to 1920, you should look for your ancestors in them.

A UNITED STATES FEDERAL CENSUS SCHEDULES
MICROFILM CABINET

UNITED STATES & CANADA INFORMATION DESK

Chapter 8

IS THERE A BIOGRAPHICAL SKETCH
ABOUT YOUR ANCESTOR?

Biographical sketches are an important secondary source for researchers searching for ancestors who have lived in the United States. Like family histories, they can provide missing clues to who, where, why, and when. Of course, a state-wide index to biographical sketches in city, county, regional, and state histories, and in biographical directories is a very useful, time-saving research tool for finding biographical sketches. By checking a name in *Michigan Biography Index* (listed below) and consulting the biographical sketches cited for that particular name, five earlier generations, including one Revolutionary War ancestor, and an earlier New England immigrant were discovered. The proliferation of biographical sketches in local, county, regional, and state histories is a unique part of the American life, mainly in the United States and some in Canada. Such a phenomenon is not the case in other countries of the world.

If the indexes listed below that may relate to your research cannot be located near your home, they should be consulted while you are at the Family History Library. The Library locations and call numbers have been provided in order to save you time looking them up while there. Some are unpublished personal indexes that may be consulted free by mail or for a small fee.

ALABAMA

Work Progress Administration. Alabama. Birmingham. "Alabama Biography: An Index to Biographical Sketches of Individual Alabamians in State, Local, and to Some Extent National Collections." Birmingham, Ala.: Birmingham Public Library, in progress.
   Contains approximately 22,500 citations of biographical sketches
   from about eighty town, county, and state histories
   and biographical directories. For mail inquiries write the
   Librarian, Tutwiler Collection of Southern History, Birmingham

Public Library, 2100 Park Place, Birmingham, AL 35203; include self-addressed stamped envelope (SASE).

The Library of Congress Index to Biographies in State and Local Histories. 31 reels of microfilm. Baltimore: Magna Carta Book Co., 1979. FHL U.S. & CAN FILM AREA 1380344 - 1380373, 1528066. Indexes eight works relating to Alabama.

Aake - Bass	1380344	Long - McCr	1380359
Bast - Booz	1380345	McCu - Mezg	1380360
Bopp - Brow	1380346	Mial - Noon	1380361
Broy-Chappel	1380347	Nor - Pizt	1380362
Chappell-Cost	1380348	Plac - Rast	1380363
Coth - Dave	1380349	Ratc - Roby	1380364
Davi - Emsw	1380350	Rocc - Schl	1380365
Enda - Flyn	1380351	Schm - Shy	1380366
Foar - Garr	1528066	Siam - Sryg	1380367
Gars - Hanz	1380352	Staa - Szol	1380368
Haon - Hely	1380353	Taaf - Triv	1380369
Heme - Hods	1380354	Trob - Wall	1380370
Hoe - Huds	1380355	Walm - Whit	1380371
Hueb-Jones, J	1380356	Whitf - Wonn	1380372
Jones, K-Lazi	1380357	Wood - Zwaa	1380373
Lea - Lone	1380358		

ALASKA

Bradbury, Connie; Hales, David A.; and Lesh, Nancy. *Alaska People Index*. Alaska Historical Commission Studies in History, no. 203. 2 vols. Anchorage: Alaska Historical Commission, 1986 (also available on 9 microfiches).

A name index to obituaries and twenty-four other sources. This book is now part of the computer database *Ancestor* that includes additional names and will continue to grow. *Ancestors* may be searched by computer through (907) 474-7261. For mail inquiries write *Ancestors*, Alaska and Polar Regions Department, Elmer E. Rasmuson Library, University of Alaska Fairbanks, Fairbanks, AK 99775-1005; include self-addressed stamped envelope.

Drazan, Joseph Gerald. *The Pacific Northwest: An Index to People and Places in Books*. Metuchen, N.J.: Scarecrow Press, 1979.
Contains 6,830 entries in 320 local history titles for Alaska, British Columbia, Idaho, Montana, Oregon, Washington and the Yukon Territory. Fifty-one titles concerning the Northwest in general and forty-seven about Alaska.

ARIZONA

Wiggins, Marvin E., comp. *Mormons and Their Neighbors: An Index to Over 75,000 Biographical Sketches from 1820 to the Present*. 2 vols. Provo, Utah: Harold B. Lee Library, Brigham Young University, 1984.
FHL LDS REG TABLE 979 D32w.
Indexes 194 titles, eleven of which are for Arizona.

The Library of Congress Index to Biographies in State and Local Histories. 31 reels of microfilm. Baltimore: Magna Carta Book Co., 1979. FHL U.S. & CAN FILM AREA 1380344 - 1380373, 1528066. See page 70 for contents of reels.
Indexes six works relating to Arizona.

ARKANSAS

"Arkansas Biographical Index." University of Arkansas.
Contains 7,500 index cards to biographical sketches of persons in state, county, city, and church histories and biographical directories, most of which were published from the 1880s to 1962. Address inquiries for only a few names at a time to Special Collections Department, University of Arkansas Libraries, Fayetteville, AR 72701. The Library charges a modest fee for making photocopies.

The Library of Congress Index to Biographies in State and Local Histories. 31 reels of microfilm. Baltimore: Magna Carta Book Co., 1979. FHL U.S. & CAN FILM AREA 1380344 - 1380373, 1528066. See page 70 for contents of reels.
Indexes ten works relating to Arkansas.

Chapter 8

CALIFORNIA

California State Library. *California Information File.* 550 microfiche.
Bellevue, Wash.: Commercial Microfilm Service, 1986.
   FHL U.S. & CAN FICHE AREA 6333977 (550 microfiche).
   Contains an estimated 1.4 million citations on approximately
   721,000 cards to periodicals, newspapers, manuscript
   collections, books, histories, theses, dissertations, government
   documents, biographical directories, and the Library's
   biographical files.

Parker, J. Carlyle. *An Index to the Biographees in 19th Century
California County Histories.* Gale Genealogy and Local History Series,
vol. 7. Detroit: Gale Research Co., 1979.
   FHL U.S. & CAN REF AREA 979.4 D32p.
   Contains approximately 16,500 entries from sixty-one county
   histories. Only four of the titles indexed in this work are not
   indexed in the *California Information File.*

COLORADO

Bromwell, Henriette Elizabeth. *Colorado Portrait and Biography
Index.* 4 vols. plus a 2 vol. supp., on 2 reels of microfilm. Denver:
n.p., 1935. Microfilmed by the Western History Department, Denver
Public Library, 1979. FHL U.S. & CAN FILM AREA 1688547 (A-
Z) - 1688548 (Appendix A-Z).
   Contains about thirty-three thousand name entries from 170 histories,
   magazines, newspapers, land records, and other records.

CONNECTICUT

"Connecticut Biography and Portrait Index." Thomas J. Kemp, Editor,
12100 Seminole Blvd. #46, Largo FL 34648, in progress.
   Contains 250,000 citations of biographical sketches from town,
   county, state, fraternal, etc., histories and photographs, sketches,
   silhouettes, and artistic portraits. The editor will search the index
   for a small fee and a self-addressed, stamped envelope.

Greenlaw, William Prescott. *The Greenlaw Index of the New England Historic Genealogical Society.* 2 vols. Boston: G. K. Hall, 1979. FHL U.S. & CAN FILM AREA Q 974 D22g.
Indexes many Connecticut and New England local histories and genealogies up to 1940.

The Library of Congress Index to Biographies in State and Local Histories. 31 reels of microfilm. Baltimore: Magna Carta Book Co., 1979. FHL U.S. & CAN FILM AREA 1380344 - 1380373, 1528066. See page 70 for contents of reels.
Indexes three works relating to Connecticut.

DELAWARE

"Surname File." Historical Society of Delaware Library.
The Library has a 500,000 card index to church records, obituaries, research files and family history files. Will search the index for a fee. Write the Library at 505 Market Street Mall, Wilmington DE 19801.

"Genealogical Surname File." Delaware State Archives.
Index to surnames in genealogies and histories. Write the Delaware State Archives, Hall of Records, Dover DE 19901 and include a self-addressed stamped envelope.

The Library of Congress Index to Biographies in State and Local Histories. 31 reels of microfilm. Baltimore: Magna Carta Book Co., 1979. FHL U.S. & CAN FILM AREA 1380344 - 1380373, 1528066. See page 70 for contents of reels.
Indexes three works relating to Delaware.

DISTRICT OF COLUMBIA

The Library of Congress Index to Biographies in State and Local Histories. 31 reels of microfilm. Baltimore: Magna Carta Book Co., 1979. FHL U.S. & CAN FILM AREA 1380344 - 1380373, 1528066. See page 70 for contents of reels.
Indexes three works relating to District of Columbia.

Chapter 8

FLORIDA

"Florida Biography Index." State Library of Florida.
Contains approximately twenty-five thousand entries to biographical sketches from town, county, and state histories; yearbooks and directories of organizations; biographical dictionaries; newspapers, and periodicals. Address inquiries to the Florida Collection, State Library of Florida, R.A. Gray Building, Tallahassee, Florida 32399-0250.

GEORGIA

The Library of Congress Index to Biographies in State and Local Histories. 31 reels of microfilm. Baltimore: Magna Carta Book Co., 1979. FHL U.S. & CAN FILM AREA 1380344 - 1380373, 1528066. See page 70 for contents of reels.
Indexes thirty-six works relating to Georgia.

HAWAII

The Library of Congress Index to Biographies in State and Local Histories. 31 reels of microfilm. Baltimore: Magna Carta Book Co., 1979. FHL U.S. & CAN FILM AREA 1380344 - 1380373, 1528066. See page 70 for contents of reels.
Indexes three works relating to Hawaii.

IDAHO

Drazan, Joseph Gerald. *The Pacific Northwest: An Index to People and Places in Books.* Metuchen, N.J.: Scarecrow Press, 1979.
Contains 6,830 entries in 320 local history titles for Alaska, British Columbia, Idaho, Montana, Oregon, Washington and the Yukon Territory. Fifty-one titles concerning the Northwest in general and thirty about Idaho.

Wiggins, Marvin E., comp. *Mormons and Their Neighbors: An Index to Over 75,000 Biographical Sketches from 1820 to the Present.* 2 vols. Provo, Utah: Harold B. Lee Library, Brigham Young University, 1984.

FHL LDS REG TABLE 979 D32w.
Indexes 194 titles, thirteen of which are for Idaho.

The Library of Congress Index to Biographies in State and Local Histories. 31 reels of microfilm. Baltimore: Magna Carta Book Co., 1979. FHL U.S. & CAN FILM AREA 1380344 - 1380373, 1528066. See page 70 for contents of reels.
Indexes twelve works relating to Idaho.

Parker, J. Carlyle, and Parker, Janet G. *Idaho Biographical and Genealogical Sketch Index.* Turlock, Calif.: Marietta Publishing Co., in progress.
Contains 24,681 index entries to the biographees in biographical and genealogical sketches in forty-four state, regional, county, and city histories and biographical directories of Idaho published between 1884 and 1982. The publisher will consult this index for researchers and provide them with bibliographic citations and page numbers, for a modest fee. Address correspondence to the Marietta Publishing Co., 2115 North Denair Avenue, Turlock CA 95380, and for this service include a self-addressed stamped envelope.

ILLINOIS

"Illinois Biographical Sketch Index." Illinois State Historical Library. Contains 135,000 index cards to biographical sketches of persons in two hundred state, county, and city histories and biographical directories. Address inquiries to the Illinois State Historical Library, Old State Capitol, Springfield, Illinois 62701.

INDIANA

Indiana Biographical Index. 16 microfiche. West Bountiful, Utah: Genealogical Indexing Associates, 1983.
FHL U.S. & CAN FICHE AREA 6331353 (16 microfiche).
Contains 247,423 name entries from 537 state, county, city, and local histories.

Chapter 8

IOWA

Morford, Charles. *Biographical Index to the County Histories of Iowa.*
Baltimore: Gateway Press, 1979.
FHL U.S. & CAN BOOK AREA 977.7 D32m.
Contains 40,540 entries of the biographees in 131 of the 251 county
histories for all of Iowa's ninety-nine counties.

KENTUCKY

Cook, Michael Lewis. *Kentucky Index of Biographical Sketches in
State, Regional, and County Histories.* Evansville, Ind.: Cook
Publications, 1986. FHL U.S. & CAN BOOK AREA 976.9 D32c.
Contains nearly seventy thousand entries to sixty-five state, regional,
and county histories.

*The Library of Congress Index to Biographies in State and Local
Histories.* 31 reels of microfilm. Baltimore: Magna Carta Book Co.,
1979. FHL U.S. & CAN FILM AREA 1380344 - 1380373,
1528066. See page 70 for contents of reels.
Indexes fifty works relating to Kentucky.

LOUISIANA

*The Library of Congress Index to Biographies in State and Local
Histories.* 31 reels of microfilm. Baltimore: Magna Carta Book Co.,
1979. FHL U.S. & CAN FILM AREA 1380344 - 1380373,
1528066. See page 70 for contents of reels.
Indexes twenty-one works relating to Louisiana.

MAINE

Estes, Marie. "Name Index to Maine Local Histories." Typescript.
Portland: Maine Historical Society Library, 1985.
This unpublished index was started in the 1940's and is added to
occasionally. Contains approximately 11,000 entries to several
hundred local histories of Maine. May be consulted by mail for
simple single requests with self-addressed stamped envelope. Mail

inquiries to Maine Historical Society Library, 485 Congress Street, Portland, ME 04101.

Maine Genealogical Society. "Surname Index to Maine Town Histories." Bar Harbor: Maine Genealogical Society, in progress. Contains approximately 14,000 entries for Maine families and settlers in Maine town histories. Write Dr. Thomas Roderick, 4 Seely Road, Bar Harbor, ME 04609 and include a self-addressed stamped envelope.

Roderick, Thomas "Name Index to Maine Families in Periodicals." Bar Harbor: The Author, in progress.
Contains approximately 13,000 entries for Maine family groups in all Maine genealogical periodicals and selected titles in the other New England states. Write Dr. Thomas Roderick, 4 Seely Road, Bar Harbor, ME 04609 and include a self-addressed stamped envelope.

MARYLAND

Andrusko, Samuel M. *Maryland Biographical Sketch Index.* Silver Spring, Md.: S. M. Andrusko, 1983.
    FHL U.S. & CAN BOOK AREA 975.2 D3a.
    Contains over 10,500 entries in thirty-three local histories.

Passano, Eleanor Phillips. *An Index of the Source Records of Maryland: Genealogical, Biographical, Historical.* Baltimore: Waverly Press, 1940. Reprint. Baltimore: Genealogical Publishing Co., 1967. Also printed in 1974 and both are the same.
    FHL U.S. & CAN BOOK AREA 975.2 D22p 1967.
    Contains an estimated twenty-five thousand entries to an estimated 5,750 sources.

MASSACHUSETTS

Greenlaw, William Prescott. *The Greenlaw Index of the New England Historic Genealogical Society.* 2 vols. Boston: G. K. Hall, 1979.
    FHL U.S. & CAN FILM AREA Q 974 D22g.

Chapter 8

Indexes many Massachusetts and New England local histories and genealogies up to 1940.

MICHIGAN

Loomis, Frances, comp. *Michigan Biography Index*. Detroit: Detroit Public Library, 1946. 4 reels of microfilm. Woodbridge, Conn.: Research Publications, 1973. FHL U.S. & CAN FILM AREA 485331, Items 4-5, 1303166 - 1303168.

Contains approximately seventy-three thousand names of the biographees in 361 biographical directories, city and county directories.

Aaga - Canf	485331, Items 4-5
Cani - Levy	1303166
Lewe - Shett	1303167
Shetz - Zynd	1303168

MINNESOTA

"Minnesota Biography Sketch Index." Minnesota Historical Society Reference Library.

The Library has two indexes of approximately 103,000 total entries to biographical sketches of persons in state, county, city and church histories; biographical directories; newspapers; and periodicals. Early index entries are primarily newspaper obituaries. Address inquiries to the Minnesota Historical Society Reference Library, 690 Cedar Street, St. Paul, MN 55101.

MISSISSIPPI

"Biographical Index." Mississippi State Department of Archives and History.

Contains approximately two hundred thousand index cards to biographical information on persons in an estimated fifty state and church histories, biographical directories, and newspapers. The index also includes entries from tax rolls, participants in the War of 1812 and Mexican War, and many state records. Address inquiries to the Mississippi State Dept. of Archives and History, P.O. Box 571, Jackson, MS 39205.

The Library of Congress Index to Biographies in State and Local Histories. 31 reels of microfilm. Baltimore: Magna Carta Book Co., 1979. FHL U.S. & CAN FILM AREA 1380344 - 1380373, 1528066. See page 70 for contents of reels.
Indexes thirteen works relating to Mississippi.

MONTANA

Parker, J. Carlyle, and Parker, Janet G. *Montana Biographical and Genealogical Sketch Index.* Turlock, Calif.: Marietta Publishing Co., in progress.
Contains 42,036 index entries to the biographees in biographical and genealogical sketches in eighty-one state, regional, county, and city histories and biographical directories of Montana published between 1894 and 1983. The publisher will consult this index for researchers and provide them with bibliographic citations and page numbers, for a modest fee. Address correspondence to the Marietta Publishing Co., 2115 North Denair Avenue, Turlock CA 95380, and for this service include a self-addressed stamped envelope.

Drazan, Joseph Gerald. *The Pacific Northwest: An Index to People and Places in Books.* Metuchen, N.J.: Scarecrow Press, 1979.
Contains 6,830 entries in 320 local history titles for Alaska, British Columbia, Idaho, Montana, Oregon, Washington and the Yukon Territory. Fifty-one titles concerning the Northwest in general and thirty-three about Montana.

NEVADA

Parker, J. Carlyle, and Parker, Janet G. *Nevada Biographical and Genealogical Sketch Index.* Turlock, Calif.: Marietta Publishing Co., 1986. FHL U.S. & CAN BOOK AREA 979.3 D32p.
Contains 7,230 index entries to the biographees in biographical and genealogical sketches in eighty-six state, regional, county, and city histories and biographical directories of Nevada published between 1870 and 1985.

Chapter 8

The Library of Congress Index to Biographies in State and Local Histories. 31 reels of microfilm. Baltimore: Magna Carta Book Co., 1979. FHL U.S. & CAN FILM AREA 1380344 - 1380373, 1528066. See page 70 for contents of reels.
Indexes eleven works relating to Nevada.

NEW HAMPSHIRE

New Hampshire Notables Card File, 1600 to the Present. 8 reels of microfilm. Salt Lake City, Utah: The Genealogical Society for the New Hampshire Historical Society, Concord, N.H., 1988.
FHL U.S. & CAN FILM AREA 1570255 - 1570262.
Contains approximately thirty-two thousand entries to collected biographies, histories, and selected New Hampshire periodicals.

Abbo - Andrews, Elisha	1570255
Andrews, Elisha - Chickering, J.B.	1570256
Chickering, J.B. - Farrington, Jeremiah	1570257
Farrington, Jeremiah - Hobart, James	1570258
Hobart, James - Mean, Robert	1570259
Mean, Robert - Richardson, Ellen Ruddick	1570260
Richardson, Ellen Ruddick-Treadwell, Thom	1570261
Treadwell, Thom-Zwicker, Kenneth Frazier	1570260

Copeley, William. *Index to Genealogies in New Hampshire Town Histories.* Concord: New Hampshire Historical Society, 1989.
FHL U.S. & CAN BOOK AREA 974.2 D22c.
An index to 302 histories from 198 towns published up to 1986. Thirty-six towns have no published histories. Only indexes surnames of families who had three generations (male or female lines) in a history. Supersedes the following:

Hunt, Elmer M. "Family Names in New Hampshire Town Histories," *Historical New Hampshire* (December 1946): 2-78.
FHL U.S. & CAN BOOK AREA 974.2 A1 no.34.
FHL U.S. & CAN FILM AREA 1033754 Item 11
FHL U.S. & CAN FICHE AREA 6046831
Contains 3,000 entries to early families from eighty-five town histories.

Copeley, William. "Family Names in New Hampshire Town Histories, 1947-1980," *Historical New Hampshire* 35 (Winter 1980): 417-39.
FHL U.S. & CAN BOOK AREA 974.2 H25n.
Supplement to Hunt's work above and indexes 180 additional town histories.

Greenlaw, William Prescott. *The Greenlaw Index of the New England Historic Genealogical Society.* 2 vols. Boston: G. K. Hall, 1979.
FHL U.S. & CAN FILM AREA Q 974 D22g.
Indexes many New Hampshire and New England local histories and genealogies up to 1940.

Towle, Glenn C. *New Hampshire Genealogical Digest, 1623-1900.*
Volume 1. Bowie, Md.: Heritage Books, 1986.
FHL U.S. & CAN BOOK AREA 974.2 D32t.
Digests numerous New Hampshire histories.

NEW YORK

"The New York State Biographical, Genealogical and Portrait Index."
Personal index of Gunther E. Pohl, 24 Walden Place,
Great Neck, NY 11020.
Includes over five hundred thousand names from over six thousand volumes, giving brief and/or extended biographical accounts and portraits appearing in New York historical resources; for example, state, county, city and town histories; church, social, Masonic, political, and military unit histories; atlases; school histories; necrologies; biographical compendiums; periodical literature; etc. Mr. Pohl will consult this index for researchers and provide them with bibliographic citations and page numbers, for a modest fee. All correspondence to him must include a SASE.

NORTH CAROLINA

The Library of Congress Index to Biographies in State and Local Histories. 31 reels of microfilm. Baltimore: Magna Carta Book Co., 1979. FHL U.S. & CAN FILM AREA 1380344 - 1380373, 1528066. See page 70 for contents of reels.
Indexes ten works relating to North Carolina.

Chapter 8

NORTH DAKOTA

Peterson, Allen. "North Dakota Biography Index." North Dakota
State University Library, Fargo, N.D.
   A twenty-seven thousand card file index to over one hundred
thousand biographical sketches in 475 titles. Mail inquiries
concerning the index to the North Dakota Institute for Regional
Studies, North Dakota State University Library, SU Station, P.O.
Box 5599, Fargo, ND 58105-5599.

*The Library of Congress Index to Biographies in State and Local
Histories.* 31 reels of microfilm. Baltimore: Magna Carta Book Co.,
1979. FHL U.S. & CAN FILM AREA 1380344 - 1380373,
1528066. See page 70 for contents of reels.
   Indexes three works relating to North Dakota.

OHIO

Ohio Historical Society. *Ohio County History Surname Index.* 64 reels
of microfilm. Columbus, Ohio: 1984.
   FHL U.S. & CAN FILM AREA 398201 - 398264.
      Contains over 450,000 names. Reels may be purchased or
   borrowed on interlibrary loan from the Ohio Historical Society,
   1982 Velma Avenue, Columbus OH 43211-2497, for a prepaid fee.

Aare - Alki	398201	Dar - Dennis	398216
All - Ashc	398202	Dennison - Doly	398217
Ashe - Ballard O.	398203	Dom - Dych	398218
Ballard, P. - Bealm	398204	Dye - Emry	398219
Beals - Bennett, R.	398205	Emso - Ferguson, L	398220
Bennett, S. - Blew	398206	Ferguson, M. - Flo	398221
Blic - Boyd, L.	398207	Floy - Frisb	398222
Boyd, M - Brown, Ab	398208	Frisc - Gear	398223
Brown, Ad - Burdg	398209	Gearh - Goode, J.	398224
Burdi - Campbell, M	398210	Goode, K - Griswol	398225
Campbell, N. - Chap	398211	Griswold - Hammon	398226
Chap - Coay	398212	Hammond - Harter	398227
Coba - Cooli	398213	Hartes - Henderson	398228
Coolm - Creighton P	398214	Henderson - Hint	398229
Creighton, R - Dan	398215	Hiny - Hoslet	398230

Hosely - Hunter, M	398231	Postley - Reams	398248
Hunter N - Jennings	398232	Reamy - Riley, N.	398249
Jennings - Kaufman	398233	Riley, N. - Row	398250
Kaufman - Kimbal	398234	Rowa - Schmitt, K.	398251
Kimbar - Koontz,	398235	Schmitt, P.-Shaw, I	398252
Koontz, Ma - Laym	398236	Shaw, J. - Sker	398253
Laymas - Linke	398237	Skid - Snyder, I.	398254
Linkh - Lydo	398238	Snyder J-Stevens, I	398255
Lync - McCracken,	398239	Stevens, I-Sunderl	398256
McCracken, L - McNe	398240	Sunderm - Thompson	398257
McNi - Mathews, Joh	398241	Thompson - Tuller	398258
Mathews, Jos-Miller	398242	Tulles - Wagner	398259
Miller, M.G.-Morra	398243	Wagner - Weaver, Ha	398260
Morre - Neuh	398244	Weaver, He-White, P	398261
Neul - Overl	398245	White, R-Wilson, F.	398262
Overm - Penni	398246	Wilson, Fa - Woolm	398263
Penno - Postlew	398247	Woolr - Zwve	398264

OKLAHOMA

The Library of Congress Index to Biographies in State and Local Histories. 31 reels of microfilm. Baltimore: Magna Carta Book Co., 1979. FHL U.S. & CAN FILM AREA 1380344 - 1380373, 1528066. See page 70 for contents of reels.
Indexes three works relating to Oklahoma.

OREGON

Drazan, Joseph Gerald. *The Pacific Northwest: An Index to People and Places in Books*. Metuchen, N.J.: Scarecrow Press, 1979.
Contains 6,830 entries in 320 local history titles for Alaska, British Columbia, Idaho, Montana, Oregon, Washington and the Yukon Territory. Fifty-one titles concerning the Northwest in general and fifty-one about Oregon.

Brandt, Patricia, and Guilford, Nancy, eds. *Oregon Biography Index*. Oregon State University Bibliographic Series, no. 11. Corvallis: Oregon State University, 1976.

Chapter 8

FHL U.S. & CAN BOOK AREA 979.5 D3b Index
FHL U.S. & CAN FILM AREA 1321470, Item 18
Contains over seventeen thousand names to biographees from forty-seven historical volumes.

PENNSYLVANIA

State Library of Pennsylvania. *Genealogical Surname Card Index.* 42 reels of microfilm. Salt Lake City, Utah: Genealogical Society, 1977.
FHL U.S. & CAN FILM AREA 1002825 Item 2 - 1002840, 1004983; 1005107 - 1005116; 1205178 - 91; 1275523
Contains an estimated forty-three thousand entries to an undetermined number of books.

A - Allen, P.	1002825 Item 2	Jord - Kett	1005110
Allen, S-Bailies	1002826	Kitt-Lawrence, A	1005111
Balliet - Bedw	1002827	Lawrence J-Longc	1005112
Bee - Boden	1002828	Longc - McDorma	1005113
Boden - Brittian	1002829	McDormo-Marshall	1005114
Brittian - Calve	1002830	Marshall-Miller S	1005115
Calvi - Clark	1002831	Miller S - Musser	1005116
Clark - Cothran	1002832	Musser - Otis	1205178
Cothran - Daven	1002833	Otis - Pidd	1205179
Daven - Dobler	1002834	Pide - Rausch	1205180
Dobler-Edlebults	1002835	Rauschb-Rockwell	1205181
Edlebults-Felty	1002836	Rockwell - Schlep	1205182
Felty - Frey, D.	1275523	Schley - Shimp	1205183
Edleblute - Fenn	1002837	Shimp - Snyder JC	1205184
Frey, E. - Gils	1002838	Snyder JC- Stone	1205185
Gils - Groves	1002839	Stone - Thomas	1205186
Groves - Hartman	1002840	Thomas - Van Dyk	1205187
Hartman - Hazell	1004983	Van Dyke - Weave	1205188
Hazell - Hobbs	1005107	Weaver - Williams	1205189
Hobbs - Humer, G	1005108	Williams - Yost D	1205190
Humer, H. - Jaco	1005109	Yost, E. - Zwoe	1205191

"Index to Pennsylvania County Histories." Carnegie Library of Pittsburgh.
A 75,000 card index to western Pennsylvanians. Two or three specific names will be searched free; with a fee if photocopies are

requested. Mail inquiries to the Carnegie Library of Pittsburgh, 4400 Forbes Avenue, Pittsburgh, PA 15213-4080.

"Pennsylvania Encyclopedia Biography Field Notes for American Guide Series." Pennsylvania Bureau of Archives and History, Harrisburg.
    FHL U.S. & CAN FILM AREA 1015709-25.
    Approximately 18,870 abstracted biographical sketches from international, national, state, and local histories and biographical directories and encyclopedias. Prepared by a Federal Writer's Project, 1939-1942.

Hoenstine, Floyd G. *Guide to Genealogical and Historical Research in Pennsylvania*. Hollidaysburg, Pa.: F.G. Hoenstine, 1978. Supplements, 1985- .
    FHL U.S. & CAN BOOK AREA 974.8 A3h 1978.
    Contains a surname index with some given names, with no page numbers, to an undetermined number of entries to 2,201 books.

RHODE ISLAND

Parker, J. Carlyle. *Rhode Island Biographical and Genealogical Sketch Index*. Turlock, Calif.: Marietta Publishing Co., 1991.
    FHL U.S. & CAN BOOK AREA 974.5 D32p.
    Contains approximately 35,000 index entries for about 19,500 biographees in 214 (364 volumes) state, regional, county, and city histories, periodical articles, newspaper articles, and histories and biographical directories of Rhode Island published between 1827 and 1989.

Greenlaw, William Prescott. *The Greenlaw Index of the New England Historic Genealogical Society*. 2 vols. Boston: G. K. Hall, 1979.
    FHL U.S. & CAN FILM AREA Q 974 D22g.
    Indexes many Rhode Island and New England local histories and genealogies up to 1940.

Chapter 8

SOUTH CAROLINA

Cote, Richard N., and Williams, Patricia H. *Dictionary of South Carolina Biography.* Vol. 1. Easley, S.C.: Southern Historical Press, 1985. FHL U.S. & CAN BOOK AREA 975.7 D36c. Contains about 13,300 entries.

The Library of Congress Index to Biographies in State and Local Histories. 31 reels of microfilm. Baltimore: Magna Carta Book Co., 1979. FHL U.S. & CAN FILM AREA 1380344 - 1380373, 1528066. See page 70 for contents of reels.
Indexes thirteen works relating to South Carolina.

SOUTH DAKOTA

Parker, J. Carlyle, and Parker, Janet G. *South Dakota Biographical and Genealogical Sketch Index.* Turlock, Calif.: Marietta Publishing Co., in progress.
Contains 19,920 index entries to the biographees in biographical and genealogical sketches in thirty-seven state, regional, county, and city histories and biographical directories of South Dakota published between 1898 and 1984. The publisher will consult this index for researchers and provide them with bibliographic citations and page numbers, for a modest fee. Address correspondence to the Marietta Publishing Co., 2115 North Denair Avenue, Turlock CA 95380, and for this service include a self-addressed stamped envelope.

TENNESSEE

The Library of Congress Index to Biographies in State and Local Histories. 31 reels of microfilm. Baltimore: Magna Carta Book Co., 1979. FHL U.S. & CAN FILM AREA 1380344 - 1380373, 1528066. See page 70 for contents of reels.
Indexes thirty-two works relating to Tennessee.

TEXAS

Ming, Virginia H., and Ming, William L. *Biographical Gazetteer of Texas: Publication of the Biographical Sketch File of the Texas*

Collection at Baylor University. 6 vols. Austin, Texas: W. M.
Morrison Books, 1985.
>   FHL U.S. & CAN BOOK AREA 976.4 D3bgt.
>   Contains over seventy thousand entries to over fifty thousand
>   individuals in 202 historical works.

*The Library of Congress Index to Biographies in State and Local
Histories.* 31 reels of microfilm. Baltimore: Magna Carta Book Co.,
1979. FHL U.S. & CAN FILM AREA 1380344 - 1380373,
1528066. See page 70 for contents of reels.
>   Indexes twenty-seven works relating to Texas.

UTAH

Wiggins, Marvin E., comp. *Mormons and Their Neighbors: An Index
to Over 75,000 Biographical Sketches from 1820 to the Present.* 2 vols.
Provo, Utah: Harold B. Lee Library, Brigham Young University, 1984.
>   FHL LDS REG TABLE 979 D32w.
>   Index to over seventy-five thousand sketches from 1820 to 1984 in
>   194 titles, thirteen of which are for Idaho and eleven for Arizona.
>   The index also covers Latter-day Saints from Canada to Mexico,
>   New York, Ohio, Missouri, and the Pacific Islands.

VERMONT

Greenlaw, William Prescott. *The Greenlaw Index of the New England
Historic Genealogical Society.* 2 vols. Boston: G. K. Hall, 1979.
>   FHL U.S. & CAN FILM AREA Q 974 D22g.
>   Indexes many Vermont and New England local histories and
>   genealogies up to 1940.

WASHINGTON

"Regional Newspaper and Washington Periodical Index." University of
Washington, Allen Library, Seattle.
>   Contains thousands of index cards to biographical sketches of persons
>   in newspapers; periodicals; some obituaries; state, county, city, and
>   church histories; and biographical directories, most of which were

published from the 1860s to date. Address inquiries for only a few names at a time to Pacific Northwest Librarian, Special Collections Division, Allen Library FM-25, University of Washington, Seattle WA 98195. All correspondence to the Librarian should include a self-addressed stamped envelope.

Drazan, Joseph Gerald. *The Pacific Northwest: An Index to People and Places in Books*. Metuchen, N.J.: Scarecrow Press, 1979.
Contains 6,830 entries in 320 local history titles for Alaska, British Columbia, Idaho, Montana, Oregon, Washington and the Yukon Territory. Fifty-one titles concerning the Northwest in general and eighty-three about Washington.

WISCONSIN

State Historical Society of Wisconsin. Library. *Subject Catalog; of the Library of the State Historical Society of Wisconsin, Madison, Wisconsin; Including the Pamphlet Subject Catalog Beginning in Volume 22*. 23 vols. Westport, Conn.: Greenwood Publishing Corp., 1971.
Contains approximately 45,000 index cards to biographical sketches of persons in state, county, city, and church histories and biographical directories. Researchers without access to this catalog or who may wish to have the 15,000 entries of sketches made since 1971 checked may write the Reference Librarian, The State Historical Society of Wisconsin, 816 State Street, Madison, WI 53706. Please give full name of person requested. Searches for all of a surname cannot be undertaken.

WYOMING

Parker, J. Carlyle, and Parker, Janet G. *Wyoming Biographical and Genealogical Sketch Index*. Turlock, Calif.: Marietta Publishing Co., in progress.
Contains 8,582 index entries to the biographees in biographical and genealogical sketches in thirty state, regional, county, and city histories and biographical directories of Wyoming published between 1899 and 1984. The publisher will consult this index for researchers and provide them with bibliographic citations and page numbers, for

a modest fee. Address correspondence to the Marietta Publishing Co., 2115 North Denair Avenue, Turlock CA 95380, and for this service include a self-addressed stamped envelope.

CANADA

BRITISH COLUMBIA

Drazan, Joseph Gerald. *The Pacific Northwest: An Index to People and Places in Books*. Metuchen, N.J.: Scarecrow Press, 1979.
Contains 6,830 entries in 320 local history titles for Alaska, British Columbia, Idaho, Montana, Oregon, Washington and the Yukon Territory. Fifty-one titles concerning the Northwest in general and forty-seven about British Columbia.

YUKON

Drazan, Joseph Gerald. *The Pacific Northwest: An Index to People and Places in Books*. Metuchen, N.J.: Scarecrow Press, 1979.
Contains 6,830 entries in 320 local history titles for Alaska, British Columbia, Idaho, Montana, Oregon, Washington and the Yukon Territory. Fifty-one titles concerning the Northwest in general and three about the Yukon.

I. FAMILY HISTORY CENTER USERS:

A few of the Family History Centers may have some of the above indexes to help you find a biographical sketch of an ancestor.

II. LOCAL PUBLIC LIBRARY USERS:

Some genealogical libraries and public libraries may also have some of the above titles.

Chapter 8

III. HOME LIBRARY USERS:

Look for newspaper obituaries and funeral programs; photocopied
sketches from biographical directories and printed histories; and
typewritten or manuscript autobiographies and biographies among your
personal papers, and write or call relatives and ask that they check their
personal papers for the same. Some of the above unpublished personal
indexes can only be consulted by mail.

SUMMARY:

Checking indexes mentioned in this chapter can reward you by adding
historical information about known ancestors and extending generations.
Prepare bibliographic cards for items of interest.

"I just found something exciting! One of those unmarriages!"

-- Researcher's conversation, overheard at
Family History Library, October 1991

Chapter 9

IS AN ANCESTOR'S NAME IN NATIONAL OR REGIONAL INDEXES?

PERIODICAL INDEXES

Genealogical and historical periodicals contain some biographical information, and some periodicals are indexed in genealogical periodical indexes. The following are a few titles that relate to the United States, with Family History Library call numbers included, that should be checked for names of interest:

Jacobus, Donald Lines. *Index to Genealogical Periodicals, 1932-1953*. Reprint. Baltimore, Genealogical Publishing Co., 1973. 3 Vols. in 1.
FHL U.S. & CAN BOOK AREA 973 B22j
FHL U.S. & CAN FILM AREA 161989

Genealogical Periodical Annual. Index. 1962-1965. Edited by Ellen Stanley Rogers. Bladensburg, Md.: Genealogical Records, 1963-1967, op.
FHL U.S. & CAN REF AREA 929.1 G286gpa.

Genealogical Periodical Annual. Index. 1966-1969. Edited by George E. Russell. Bowie, Md.: The Author, 1966-1973, op.
FHL U.S. & CAN REF AREA 929.1 G286gpa.

Genealogical Periodical Annual. Index. 1974- Edited by Laird C. Towle, Bowie, Md.: The Heritage Books, 1976- .
FHL U.S. & CAN REF AREA 929.1 G286gpa.

Periodical Source Index (PERSI). 1847-1985. Prepared by the Staff of the Allen County Public Library, Genealogy Department, Fort Wayne, Indiana. Edited by Anne Dallas Budd, Michael Barren Clegg, and Curt Bryan Witcher. Fort Wayne, Ind.: The Foundation, 1988.
FHL U.S. & CAN REF AREA 973 D25per & FHCs 6016863.

Chapter 9

Periodical Source Index (PERSI). 1986- Prepared by the Staff of the Allen County Public Library, Genealogy Department, Fort Wayne, Indiana. Fort Wayne, Ind.: Allen County Public Library Foundation, 1987- .

> FHL U.S. & CAN REF AREA 973 D25per & FHCs 6016864.
> Available at many libraries and Centers of the Family History Library. If the Family History Library does not have any periodical titles of interest, an easy way to obtain copies of articles listed in the PERSI index is for the researcher to order photocopies from the Allen County Public Library, P.O. Box 2270, Ft. Wayne, IN 46801, as they hold all of the titles indexed. You should provide the index entry from PERSI for not more than eight articles at a time. The Allen County Public Library will bill patrons $3.00 for each letter, plus 20 cents per page photocopied. Because there are no page numbers given in the index, it is impossible to estimate the cost of photocopying. You should not request articles by telephone or FAX.

Additional titles of cumulative indexes to individual periodicals are listed in Kip Sperry's *A Survey of American Genealogical Periodicals and Periodical Indexes* (Detroit: Gale Research Co, 1978. FHL U.S. & CAN BOOK AREA 973 B23s).

If you find an article of interest in any of the above periodical indexes, prepare a bibliographic card for it and consult the *Family History Library Catalog: Author/Title Catalog* for that periodical title. When you find the call number in the *Catalog*, add it to your bibliographic card.

There are many periodicals that are not indexed, and it may be useful to browse through such titles as time permits while at the Family History Library. If you do not know the name of a genealogical or historical periodical for a specific geographical location, you may find some in the *Family History Library Catalog: Locality Catalog* by using the following periodicals subject headings subdivisions for a state:

State-wide periodicals:
  CALIFORNIA - ARCHIVES AND LIBRARIES - PERIODICALS
  CALIFORNIA - GENEALOGY - PERIODICALS

CALIFORNIA - GENEALOGY - SOCIETIES - PERIODICALS
CALIFORNIA - HISTORY - PERIODICALS
CALIFORNIA - HISTORY - SOCIETIES - PERIODICALS
CALIFORNIA - MINORITIES - GENEALOGY - PERIODICALS
CALIFORNIA - NATIVE RACES - PERIODICALS
CALIFORNIA - PERIODICALS
CALIFORNIA - SOCIETIES - PERIODICALS

County periodicals:
CALIFORNIA, AMADOR - GENEALOGY - SOCIETIES -
PERIODICALS
CALIFORNIA, EL DORADO - PERIODICALS
CALIFORNIA, STANISLAUS - HISTORY - SOCIETIES -
PERIODICALS

City periodicals:
CALIFORNIA, FRESNO, REEDLEY - HISTORY -
PERIODICALS

The above examples are taken from the California portion of the *Family History Library Catalog: Locality Catalog.* There may be a few additional subject headings used for other states and foreign countries. However, the last subdivision will always be PERIODICALS.

Periodicals of nationwide interest and scope are found in the *Family History Library Catalog: Subject Catalog* under the subject heading GENEALOGY - PERIODICALS and also in the *Family History Library Catalog: Locality Catalog* under the subject headings:
MEXICO - GENEALOGY - PERIODICALS
UNITED STATES - GENEALOGY - PERIODICALS

U.S. NATIONWIDE INDEXES

The following nationwide indexes for the United States are listed in order of importance according to the value judgment of the author:

93

Chapter 9

American Genealogical-Biographical Index to American Genealogical, Biographical and Local History Materials. Middletown, Conn.: Godfrey Memorial Library, 1952- in progress.
FHL U.S. & CAN BOOK AREA 973 D22ag.

> Clark, Patricia I. and Huntsman, Dorothy, eds. *Key Title Index to the American Genealogical-Biographical Index: Register of Family History Library Call Numbers.* Salt Lake City: FHL, 1990.
> FHL U.S. & CAN BOOK AREA 973 D22am Index.
> Microfiche. Salt Lake City, GSU, 1992. FHL U.S. & CAN FICHE AREA 6088377 (1 microfiche).
> Includes the book and microform numbers for the books indexed that are available in the Family History Library.

Newberry Library, Chicago. *The Genealogical Index.* 4 Vols. Boston: G.K. Hall, 1960. FHL U.S. & CAN REF AREA Q 929 N424g. Available from FHL through FHC: microfilm 928135-928137.
> Contains 512,000 entries, indexed between 1896 and 1917.

California. State Library, Sacramento. Sutro Branch, San Francisco. *The Surname Catalog.* 3rd. ed. Sacramento: California State Library Foundation, 1990.
> Good for family histories, includes individuals, and is nationwide in coverage. Over fifty thousand entries to 12,000 family histories and other books (also includes *State and Local History Catalog* and *Miscellaneous Catalog*)

Brown, Stuart E., Jr., comp. *Virginia Genealogies, A Trial List of Printed Books and Pamphlets.* Berryville, Va.: Virginia Book Co., 1967.
> FHL U.S. & CAN BOOK AREA 975.5 D23b v.1.
> Cites 1,962 family histories and gives numerous "see references" in its index.

Index to American Genealogies; and to Genealogical Material Contained in All Works as Town Histories, County Histories, Local Histories, Historical Society Publications, Biographies, Historical Periodical and Kindred Works. 5th ed. rev. Albany, N.Y.: Munsell, 1900, 1908. Reprint. Baltimore: Genealogical Pub. Co., 1967.

FHL U.S. & CAN REF AREA 929.173 IN2a
FHL U.S. & CAN FICHE AREA 6051301 (6 microfiche)
FHL U.S. & CAN FILM AREA 599811

The American Genealogist, Being a Catalogue of Family Histories. A Bibliography of American Genealogy, or a List of the Title Pages of Books and Pamphlets on Family History, Published in America, from 1771 to Date. 5th ed. Albany: Munsell, 1900. Reprint. Detroit: Gale Research Co., 1975. Baltimore: Genealogical Pub. Co., 1967.
　　FHL U.S. & CAN REF AREA 973 D23am 1900.
　　This work and the *Index to American Genealogies* (see above) should be used together. The *American Genealogist* is, in part, a bibliography of the family histories indexed in the *Index to American Genealogies.*

Kirkham, E. Kay. *An Index to Some of the Bibles and Family Records of the United States: (Excluding the Southern States); 45,000 References as Taken from the Microfilm at the Genealogical Society of Utah.* Volume II. Logan, Utah: Everton, 1984.
　　FHL U.S. & CAN BOOK AREA 973 D22kk v.2.

The Library of Congress Index to Biographies in State and Local Histories. 31 reels of microfilm. Baltimore: Magna Carta Book Co., 1979. FHL U.S. & CAN FILM AREA 1380344 - 1380373, 1528066. See page 70 for contents of reels.
　　Contains approximately 170,000 entries to biographees of some volumes in the Library of Congress. It indexes only 340 titles. Kentucky has the largest number of titles indexed with 50; Georgia has 36; California, 34; Tennessee, 32; Texas, 27; Louisiana, 21; Mississippi, 13; South Carolina, 13; Idaho, 12; Nevada, 11; Arkansas, 10; North Carolina, 10; Alabama, 8; Arizona, 6; and all other states, 3 or less.

McMullin, Phillip W., ed. *Grassroots of America; A Computerized Index to the American State Papers: Land Grants and Claims (1789-1837) with Other Aids to Research.* Salt Lake City: Gendex Corp., 1972.
　　FHL U.S. & CAN REF AREA 973 R2m
　　FHL & FHCs U.S. & CAN FICHE AREA 6051333

Chapter 9

This index is simply a personal name index to the sections of public land and claims in the *American State Papers*. Index entries are to the *American State Papers*, volumes 1-9 which are available on FHL U.S. & CAN FILM AREA 899878-85 or 908743-50. The following table converts the volume numbers into *American State Papers* Serial Set numbers:

	Index Entry no.	Serial Set	FHL no.
Public Lands	1	028	899878 or 908743
Public Lands	2	029	899879 or 908744
Public Lands	3	030	899880 or 908745
Public Lands	4	031	899881 or 908746
Public Lands	5	032	899882 or 908747
Public Lands	6	033	899883 or 908748
Public Lands	7	034	899884 or 908749
Public Lands	8	035	899885 or 908750
Claims	9	036	944495

In many cases the information found in the *American State Papers* is nothing more than a petition list or a list of landholders. However, the location and date are usually given; and these are useful for continued research, particularly if a county was previously unknown.

REGIONAL INDEXES

Southern States

Kirkham, E. Kay. *An Index to Some of the Family Records of the Southern States: 35,000 Microfilm References from the N.S.D.A.R. Files and Elsewhere.* Logan, Utah: Everton Publishers, 1979.
> FHL U.S. & CAN BOOK AREA 973 D22kk v.1.
> Indexes Bibles, family records, and family histories. Entries refer to the microfilm reel numbers of the Family History Library.

Leon S. Hollingsworth Genealogical Card File.
FHL U.S. & CAN FILM AREA 1308005 - 1308007.
Contains approximately 297,000 given names. Covers research concerning persons from throughout the Southeast, primarily Georgia, but also including North and South Carolina, Virginia, and Alabama.

Stewart, Robert Armistead. *Index to Printed Virginia Genealogies, Including Key and Bibliography.* Richmond, Va.: Old Dominion Press, 1930. Reprint. Baltimore: Genealogical Publishing Co., 1970.
FHL U.S. & CAN BOOK AREA 975.5 D22s
FHL U.S. & CAN FILM AREA 962558, Item 2
FHL U.S. & CAN FICHE AREA 6019375
The author includes anyone from Virginia listed in any book he checked in his nationwide search for Virginians.

New England

Greenlaw, William Prescott. *The Greenlaw Index of the New England Historic Genealogical Society.* 2 vols. Boston: G. K. Hall, 1979.
FHL U.S. & CAN REF Q AREA 974 D22g.
Contains over thirty-five thousand entries. Indexes genealogical works; family histories; state, county, and city histories; biographical directories; and periodicals acquired by the society between 1900 and 1940. Entries are limited to families for which three or more generations are reported in a work.

Middle Atlantic States

Genealogical Society of Pennsylvania. *Genealogical Material Index: The Manuscript Card Catalogue of the Historical and Genealogical Societies of Pennsylvania.* Salt Lake City: Genealogical Department of the Church of Jesus Christ of Latter-day Saints, 1967.
FHL U.S. & CAN FILM AREA 377629 - 377637.
The collections indexed in this source represent many of the Eastern Seaboard states, England and Nassau, but mainly the states

of Pennsylvania and New Jersey. The guide that follows this entry must be used with this index in order to convert the call numbers of most of the large manuscript collections on the index cards to a Family History Library microfilm reel number. All of the microfilm for the above index and the materials indexed (over one thousand reels) may be borrowed through Family History Centers.

Index A-B	377629	Index L	337634
Index C	337630	Index M-P	377635
Index D	377631	Index Q-S	337636
Index E-G	337632	Index T-Z	337637
Index H-K	337633		

Parker, J. Carlyle. *Pennsylvania and Middle Atlantic States Genealogical Manuscripts: A User's Guide to the Manuscript Collections of the Genealogical Society of Pennsylvania as Indexed in Its Manuscript Materials Index Microfilmed by the Genealogical Department, Salt Lake City.* Turlock, Calif.: Marietta Publishing Co., 1986.
  FHL U.S. & CAN BOOK AREA 974.8 D27pp.
  It is essential that this guide be used with the above index. After this guide was prepared the Family History Library recataloged the index and renamed it *Genealogical Material Index*, replacing the name *Manuscript Materials Index*.

Pacific Northwest

Drazan, Joseph Gerald. *The Pacific Northwest: An Index to People and Places in Books.* Metuchen, N.J.: Scarecrow Press, 1979.
  Contains 6,830 entries in 320 local history titles for Alaska, British Columbia, Idaho, Montana, Oregon, Washington and the Yukon Territory.

Prepare bibliographic cards for all books and articles found to be of interest in the above sources.

I. FAMILY HISTORY CENTER USERS:

Some of the titles in this chapter are available in some Family History Centers.

II. LOCAL PUBLIC LIBRARY USERS:

Some of the above titles may be available in local public libraries. Your library may also have some of the following indexes to national and international biographical directories:

Bio-Base: A Periodic Cumulative Master Index on Microfiche to Sketches Found in About 500 Current and Historical Biographical Dictionaries, 1984; Master Cumulation. Microfiche. Detroit: Gale Research Co., 1984, or *Biography and Genealogy Master Index* (Detroit: Gale Research Co., 1980- , or *Abridged Biography and Genealogy Master Index: A Consolidated Index to More Than 1,600,000 Biographical Dictionaries Indexed in Biography and Genealogy and Master Index Through 1987.* Detroit: Gale Research Co., 1988.
   FHL   U.S. & CAN REF AREA   016.92 G131 no.1.

Hyamson, Albert Montefiore. *A Dictionary of Universal Biography of All Ages and of All Peoples.* 3d ed., entirely rewritten. New York: Dutton, 1951. Reprint. Detroit: Gale Research Co., 1980.
   Contains index entries to over 110,000 persons in twenty-four early twentieth century biographical dictionaries and encyclopedias.

Riches, Phyllis M. *An Analytical Bibliography of Universal Collected Biography, Comprising Books Published in the English Tongue in Great Britain and Ireland, America and the British Dominions.* London: The Library Association, 1934. Reprint. New York: Johnson Reprint Corp., 1973. Reprint. Detroit: Gale Research Co., 1980.
   Contains over fifty-six thousand index entries to biographical sketches in over three thousand biographies published through 1933.

Phillips, Lawrence Barnett. *The Dictionary of Biographical Reference; Containing Over One Hundred Thousand Names; Together with a*

Chapter 9

Classed Index of the Biographical Literature of Europe and America.
New ed., rev., cor. and augm. with supplement to date, by Frank
Weitenkampf. London: S. Low, Marston and Co., 1889. Reprint.
Graz, Austria: Akade-mische, Druck-u Verlagsanstalt, 1966.
An index to forty-two nineteenth century biographical dictionaries
and encyclopedias.

III. HOME LIBRARY USERS:

Those indexes among the above titles that may be of interest to you
should be checked for your surnames while you are researching at the
Family History Library.

ADDITIONAL READING:

Parker, J. Carlyle. "Genealogical Name Indexes," chapter 9, pages
119-24; and "Genealogical Periodicals and Periodical Indexes," chapter
10, pages 125-29. In *Library Service for Genealogists*. Gale
Genealogy and Local History Series, vol. 15. Detroit: Gale Research
Co, 1981, op. FHL U.S. & CAN REF AREA 026.9291 P226L. 2d
edition in progress by Marietta Publishing Co.

SUMMARY:

As time permits, the appropriate national and regional indexes listed in
this chapter can be helpful in your search for information concerning
ancestors. Prepare bibliographic cards for sources that indexes indicate
deal with ancestors of interest.

Chapter 10

WHAT TO TAKE?

A reader responded to our survey on how to improve the second edition by asking for suggestions on what to take to Salt Lake City for research. Below is a list of what the author believes is essential.

However, I once made a research trip abroad almost empty-handed. Many years ago I had the opportunity to do a couple of days of research in the county archives of Surrey, in Guildford, and Hampshire, in Winchester, England. Long before going, I used the parish registers available at the Family History Library and through its Family History Centers, and determined that the Library did not have microfilm of all of the registers that were needed. Because baggage was limited in poundage and the trip involved four weeks of sedan travel in nine countries, research papers were limited to as few as needed. After some analysis the necessary research information was penned on eleven three by five cards and note paper was purchased in England. The end result was a very successful research trip which far exceeded the prepared research objectives and priorities.

The following is a prioritized list of what is recommended for a research trip to the Family History Library:

Checklist of research and personal items to be checked off as you pack
  (example: pedigree sheets, paper clips, tooth brush, comb, etc.)
Your copy of *Going to Salt Lake City to Do Family History Research*
Cards or computer printouts of ancestral research needs, objectives,
  and priorities
Pedigree sheets related to needs, objectives, and priorities
Family group sheets related to needs, objectives, and priorities
Research logs (or equivalent) related to needs, objectives, and
  priorities
Correspondence logs related to needs, objectives, and priorities
Note paper, 3"x5" cards and 3"x5" pad of note paper (free 8½"x11"
  scratch paper is available in limited quantities at the Library)

Chapter 10

Return address stickers or a rubber stamp for marking ownership of
　　research notes and photocopies
Sticky notes (self-stick removable notes):　Caution, they leave residue.
　　Please do not place them in books or on microforms, on your
　　original documents, or attach to photographs.
Pencils and pens
Extra manila file folders or ring binder dividers for families,
　　persons, or places
Paper clips
Rubber bands
Case (not a box) for 3"x5" cards (a bank passbook case works for some
　　researchers)
Sweater for cold spots in the Library both summer and winter
Briefcase or canvas bag
Magnifying glass
Stapler and staples
Coin purse with strap or waist pack (women's clothing without pockets)
Ear plugs for those unfortunate occasions when you are reading near
　　other researchers who make too much noise

Leave at home:

Original documents, certificates, licenses
Research papers that do not relate to research objectives

SUMMARY

Travel as light and as comfortably as possible.　Please don't take your
two-draw file cabinet, it is hard on other patrons' shins.

PART II

WHEN YOU'RE THERE

Chapter 11

AT THE FAMILY HISTORY LIBRARY

It is very important that you read all of this chapter and chapter 12 before going to the Family History Library. The information covered in both chapters is essential for your efficient use of the Library.

The Library is located at 35 North West Temple Street next to JB's Restaurant and the Howard Johnson Hotel on the south, the Salt Lake valley's first log cabin and the Church History Museum on the north, and Temple Square on the East. The Library is shown as number 3 on the attractions map on the inside back cover of this work.

Some researchers advocate that an orientation to the Library is helpful. Orientation is offered to the left of the main entrance lobby.

If you have decided to orient yourself, find the floor on which your books, microfilm, and microfiche are located (see list below). If you have already used the *Family History Library Catalog* in a Family History Center, upon arrival at your floor of research interest, take out your prioritized bibliographic cards or computer printouts and find the first item in the collection. If you still need to consult the *Family History Library Catalog*, take your geographical, individual, family surname cards, and cards of ancestral research needs in priority order and look up the call numbers for the research materials needed as explained in chapters 5 and 6.

You will need to approach the Library's collection geographically, except for family histories, which are alphabetical, and microforms which are filed by number. Both books and microfilm are located together on their respective floors, except for Canada and the United States. The organization of the collection, including Dewey Decimal Classification Scheme numbers, is by the following areas of research, which are located on the indicated floors of the Family History Library:

Africa	960-968	Basement 1
Asia	950-959	Basement 1

British Isles	941-942	Basement 2
Canada Books	971	Main Floor
Canada Family		
History Books	929.2	Main Floor
Canada Microforms		Second Floor
Europe	943-949	Basement 1
Latin America	972 980	Basement 1
Middle East	955-956	Basement 1
Oceania	969 990	Basement 1
Scandinavia	948	Basement 1
United States Books	973-979	Main Floor
United States Family		
History Books	929.2	Main Floor
United States Microforms		Second Floor

If it is difficult to find a microfilm reader or table space on the U.S. and Canada floors of the Library, there are usually microfilm readers and table space available on the lower levels of the Library, and you are allowed to take your books and microfilm there. Please do not take more than five books or microforms at one time, and, when you are finished with them, return them to the floor where you found them. Books should be returned to the red shelves at the end of the range of shelving from which you removed them. Make sure that you refile your microfilms and that they are refiled in the correct place. Microfiche are refiled by library attendants. Please place microfiche in the baskets on top of the microfiche cabinets.

When leaving microfilm readers for lunch, dinner, or anytime for more than thirty minutes, the Library staff requests that researchers remove their materials in order for others to use the readers. Library attendants may remove unattended materials left by a microfilm reader for longer than thirty minutes.

Reference books are shelved near the Information Desk on each floor and include the most-often-used titles, such as gazetteers, atlases, indexes, and bibliographies. Bound state-wide United States federal census schedule indexes are shelved on reference tables on the second floor near the reference desk, where they are most useful. *FamilySearch* computers are available on all floors and will be in the

historic Hotel Utah building *FamilySearch* Center, South Temple and
Main Streets (number 8 on the attractions map on the inside back
cover of this work). The oversize or folio collection consists of larger
or taller-than-average books shelved at the beginning of the U.S. book
collection on the second floor and at the end of the British book
collection in basement 2. They are usually shelved at the end of other
foreign countries' collections. Oversize book call numbers are
preceded with a capital letter "Q".

While doing research at the Family History Library, review research
needs. Review may help you keep your sights on your research
objectives. Remember to ask yourself: "Is this part of my research
really necessary?"

BROWSING

Browsing may distract from your research objectives and you should
not overindulge in it; but it can be a useful part of using a library. It is
difficult to browse in most genealogical libraries because books are not
on the shelves in alphabetical order by country, state, or county.
However, the Family History Library facilitates easier browsing in its
book collection than in most libraries through the use of its library
subject classification scheme. The second line of the call number on
the spine of the book identifies the subject contents of the book. The
letter and the digit, "V2," on the second line of the call number, for
example, means that the book contains vital records. This means that
some vital records of Shelby County, Ohio abstracted, published, and
added to the Library's collection, have the following call number:

977.145
V2ab

Similarly, "K2" is used for church records of births, christenings,
marriages, and deaths. Church records of Bloomfield Township,
Bedford County, Pennsylvania abstracted and published, would be
assigned the following call number:

974.871/B1
K2b

"P2" is used for wills and probate records. The wills and probate records of Jefferson County, Iowa, abstracted and published, are labeled with the following call number:

977.794
P2j

The above and additional selected subject classification scheme numbers that may be of interest are listed below by both subject and number:

Biography	D3
Cemetery records	V3
Church records	K2
City directories	E4
City histories	H2
County histories	H2
Court records	P2
Genealogical periodicals B2 or D25*	
Genealogies	D2
Minority histories	F2
Land and property	R2
Military records	M2
Naturalization	P4
Probate records	P2
School records	J2
Ship passenger lists	W3
Societies	C4
State histories	H2
Tax records	R4
Vital records	V2
Voting records	N4
Wills	P2

B3 or D25	Genealogical periodicals*
C4	Societies
D2	Genealogies
D3	Biography
E4	City directories
F2	Minority histories
H2	City, county, and/or state histories

J2	School records
K2	Church records
M2	Military records
N4	Voting records
P2	Court and probate records, and wills
P4	Naturalization
R2	Land and property
R4	Tax records
V2	Vital records
V3	Cemetery records
W3	Ship passenger lists
X2	Census schedules

* The B2 category is for general periodicals but was also used for genealogical periodicals for many years. The D25 category is now used for genealogical periodicals, but many genealogical periodicals still remain under the B2 category.

GENEALOGY BOOK CALL NUMBERS

Chapter 11

DEWEY DECIMAL CLASSIFICATION SCHEME

The Family History Library utilizes the Dewey Decimal Classification Scheme, which does not arrange states on the library shelves in alphabetical order, Alabama through Wyoming, but places the books geographically by state, starting with Maine westward to Hawaii.

The following is a numerical list of beginning numbers of the arrangement of states in the Dewey Decimal Classification Scheme:

974.1	Maine	976.9	Kentucky
974.2	New Hampshire	977.1	Ohio
974.3	Vermont	977.2	Indiana
974.4	Massachusetts	977.3	Illinois
974.5	Rhode Island	977.4	Michigan
974.6	Connecticut	977.5	Wisconsin
974.7	New York	977.6	Minnesota
974.8	Pennsylvania	977.7	Iowa
974.9	New Jersey	977.8	Missouri
975.1	Delaware	978.1	Kansas
975.2	Maryland	978.2	Nebraska
975.3	District of	978.3	South Dakota
	Columbia	978.4	North Dakota
975.4	West Virginia	978.6	Montana
975.5	Virginia	978.7	Wyoming
975.6	North Carolina	978.8	Colorado
975.7	South Carolina	978.9	New Mexico
975.8	Georgia	979.1	Arizona
975.9	Florida	979.2	Utah
976.1	Alabama	979.3	Nevada
976.2	Mississippi	979.4	California
976.3	Louisiana	979.5	Oregon
976.4	Texas	979.6	Idaho
976.6	Oklahoma	979.7	Washington
976.7	Arkansas	979.8	Alaska
976.8	Tennessee	996.9	Hawaii

In general, the arrangement of states begins in the Northeast with Maine and works south down the Atlantic Coast, and then with variations of south to north and north to south, westward to the Pacific Coast and Hawaii. The counties within a state are also in various geographical arrangements and not in alphabetical order.

For researchers who would prefer a list with an alphabetical approach, here is a list of the Dewey Decimal Classification Scheme in alphabetical order by state:

State	Code	State	Code
Alabama	976.1	Missouri	977.8
Alaska	979.8	Montana	978.6
Arizona	979.1	Nebraska	978.2
Arkansas	976.7	Nevada	979.3
California	979.4	New Hampshire	974.2
Colorado	978.8	New Jersey	974.9
Connecticut	974.6	New Mexico	978.9
Delaware	975.1	New York	974.7
District of		North Carolina	975.6
Columbia	975.3	North Dakota	978.4
Florida	975.9	Ohio	977.1
Georgia	975.8	Oklahoma	976.6
Hawaii	996.9	Oregon	979.5
Idaho	979.6	Pennsylvania	974.8
Illinois	977.3	Rhode Island	974.5
Indiana	977.2	South Carolina	975.7
Iowa	977.7	South Dakota	978.3
Kansas	978.1	Tennessee	976.8
Kentucky	976.9	Texas	976.4
Louisiana	976.3	Utah	979.2
Maine	974.1	Vermont	974.3
Maryland	975.2	Virginia	975.5
Massachusetts	974.4	Washington	979.7
Michigan	977.4	West Virginia	975.4
Minnesota	977.6	Wisconsin	977.5
Mississippi	976.2	Wyoming	978.7

Chapter 11

ETIQUETTE FOR THE LIBRARY

There are numerous rules of etiquette and principles of common sense that should be followed in the Library. Both underlining and check-marking with pens on microform reading machine screens and surfaces are a nuisance to others. When using library materials special care should be taken not to mark, mutilate, dog-ear corners, deface, finger lick (to turn pages), nor to place note paper on book pages while taking notes. When photocopying books be careful not to push down so hard on the spines that the bindings break. When other researchers are waiting in line for photocopying, please limit yourself to five copies at a time, then move to the end of the line if you have additional copies to make.

Research materials should be limited to five items removed from shelves or microform drawers at a time. Rewind the microfilm back onto the reel that was in the box. Spreading papers across a table into the area where others may need to work can be as annoying and inconsiderate as talking loudly or constantly to others or oneself. Helping to maintain a quiet library atmosphere is the responsibility of all researchers. On a recent visit to the Library one gentleman was wearing ear plugs. Not a bad idea when others nearby are making too much noise.

Please be careful of pet phrases or oaths which may be offensive to researchers seated next to you. Modest dress is also a courtesy in any library. Library policy requires that children under twelve be kept under control. The Family History Library does not have a children's collection and children may find the Library boring.

FAMILY GROUP RECORDS COLLECTION

Another project that should not be overlooked while at the Family History Library is to search for your ancestors in the *Family Group Records Collection* (*FGRC*). This collection contains approximately eight million family group sheets representing research submitted by LDS Church members from 1942 to 1969. Its contents cover twentieth century families back to the sixteenth century. Some group sheets contain errors; nevertheless, the search should be made.

The collection is arranged in alphabetical order by the surname and given names of the father of each family and further sub-arranged by the birth date of the fathers for names that are the same. The cards or computer lists for individuals which you prepared as a part of chapter 1 can be used to check the *Family Group Records Collection*.

The *Family Group Records Collection* is available on microfilm and is located on the second floor. It consists of many parts, the largest of which is the *Family Group Records Collection: Archive Section*, which was collected from members of the Church of Jesus Christ of Latter-day Saints from 1942-1969, but represents families from about 1500-1969. There are two microfilm sets of this collection. While at the Family History Library it is best to read the 35mm microfilm copy (1060000-1063691). The 16mm microfilm (1273501-1275491) may circulate to Family History Centers. The data in the *Family Group Records Collection* will eventually be added as another file in *FamilySearch*. The original records are still available on Basement 2 of the Library; however, they are not as complete as the microfilm, as over the years records have been removed from them.

HELP - FIXING AND OPERATING MACHINES - LOCATING BOOKS AND MICROFORMS

If equipment fails, documents are not understandable, or a different size lens is needed for a microform reading machine or printer, ask for help at the Library Attendant's Window or Station adjacent to the Copy Center on each floor. Examples of other problems that should be brought to the attention to the Library Attendants are difficulties finding books or microforms, burned out reader bulbs, and mechanical problems with readers or copy machines. They may also be able to locate duplicate copies of microfilm that may be lost or misplaced.

Library Attendants will help you with everything but research questions. If the Library Attendants' Stations personnel or librarians or

Chapter 11

volunteers at the Information Desk are too busy at the moment and you must wait in line, pick up some work to do while waiting in line.

HELP - REFERENCE AND/OR RESEARCH

Go to the Information Desk for research help. Write down the suggestions that the librarian makes concerning research problems.

If a particular book is confusing, check the introduction or preface for an explanation of how it is organized or how to use it. After having read and studied the introduction and preface, if you are still confused, consult a librarian at the Information Desk. In the front of most books there is usually also a list of abbreviations used that you may find helpful.

Also read "Reference Questions: How to Ask Them" and "Reference Service" in this chapter.

MAPS

If you need to consult some maps while at the Family History Library, check the *Family History Library Catalog: Locality Catalog* under your geographical place of interest with the subject heading subdivision, "MAPS:"

OHIO, ROSS, CHILLICOTHE - MAPS

The United States and Canada maps are shelved in locked cases to the right of the Special Collections Room on the main floor. Provide the Library Attendants in their Station adjacent to the Copy Center with the call number and title of the map. The attendant will open the cases and locate the map for you. Foreign maps are on their respective floors. Sample call numbers are as follows:

U.S. & CAN	BRITISH	EUROPE
MAP CASE	MAP CASE	MAP CASE
970	942.85	946
E7cm	E7c	E7mc

MICROFORMS

Microform collections are shelved near their reading machines.
Microforms include microfiche and 35mm and 16mm reel microfilm.
Microfiche catalogs and indexes are also located near the Information
Desk on each floor.

The basic parts of microfilm reading machines are the loading
apparatus, focus device, hand crank or motor switch, and the margin
device. The margin device, sometimes called a scanning device,
moves the microfilm from side to side under the lens and thereby
moves the image on the reading surface.

If, after experimenting with the machine, you are unable to discover
these parts or how they work, make sure that you ask someone for
assistance. A fellow researcher may be able to help and save the time
that it might take to find a Library Attendant to help you. If a
microform is difficult to read, it may be a little easier to read on a
different reading machine. Often the len sizes are not standard on
reading machines, the brightness of the lamps differ, lamps grow dim
with age, and the clarity of microfilm readers also differs because of
dust and scratches on the glass plates.

Microfilm in a one inch box is 16mm. Microfilm in an 1 5/8" thick
box is 35mm. Usually, both 16mm and 35mm may be used on a
regular reader. However, if the reader you are using is incapable of
enlarging the film's image enough for your reading comfort, move to a
reader with zoom or a higher magification. Some of these readers are
labeled "Adjustable Magnification," "High Magnification," "Zoom
Lens," "42X," or "65X." If a reader or table space is not available on
the floor where your materials are located, you may take the material to
another floor for use. There is usually space available on the 1st and 2d
basement floors.

PEDIGREE FILE

Family History Library Catalog includes entries for materials identified
as in the "PEDIGREE FILE," which is located in locked cases to the
right and left of the Special Collections Room on the main floor.

Chapter 11

REFERENCE QUESTIONS: HOW TO ASK THEM

Some researchers have difficulty asking the right questions for the help that they need. The successful reference question is specific, to the point, and is a short explanation of what is really needed. Genealogical reference questions are usually best accompanied by a pedigree, along with supporting family group sheets for each couple on the pedigree, that can be shown to a reference librarian as needed. Quantities of unorganized notes, letters, certificates, etc., piled upon the Information Desk create confusion.

Don't hesitate to ask a question, but try to ask for the right thing. Often asking for a specific book or type of material, such as, "Do you have a history of Queen Annes County, Maryland?" may meet with a negative answer or with a referral to the *Family History Library Catalog: Locality Catalog*. On the other hand, a question with a short explanation that you need to find the names of the father and mother of an ancestor born in Barclay, Queen Annes County, Maryland in 1789, may bring a reference to a source that will answer the question. These comments are offered to assist you, not to intimidate you from asking questions.

Please do not tell the librarian your complete family history or ask at one time all of the questions that relate to your research needs. Another good point to remember is that librarians, being human, need time to ponder and think about a problem. They may even need quiet time to analyze a difficult problem. Please remember how distracting a talkative child can be when you need time to concentrate on a problem.

Librarians have limited time to help each patron and cannot go through the details of all of your research. Learn to research as independently as possible. Try to think through all problems alone; then if you cannot solve them, ask for help.

Another distracting factor, though it may not appear so to a researcher, is the continuous stating of your relationship to the person for whom you are searching, such as, "my maternal great, great grandmother." Usually librarians do not find that helpful, and often much time is spent by researchers simply trying to keep the relationships straight. It is more efficient just to use the name and show where the ancestor is on a pedigree.

REFERENCE SERVICE

The reference desks at the Family History Library, as well as at many libraries, are called Information Desks. They are on all research floors of the Library. Usually there is a full-time genealogist or genealogical librarian on duty at all times, assisted by volunteers. If you are not satisfied with an answer to your question, ask if there is someone to whom you may be referred concerning your question. There are many additional specialists who are working in their offices, who may be called upon, when necessary, to address difficult questions. There is also an Information Desk (not a reference desk) in the lobby of the Library entrance on the main floor.

Also, the Library prepares very useful "Research Outlines" for each state of the United States and many foreign countries. If you have not already read the "Research Outlines" of the geographical area of research that you are pursuing, it should be read soon after you arrive in Salt Lake City. Even if you had read it beforehand you should review it again and again while in Salt Lake City. They are on display near each Information Desk and available for purchase in the Copy Centers.

RESEARCH NOTES

Research notes should include the author, title, date of publication, publisher, book call number or microform number, and page of the book or microform where information was found. The date and the library where the data was found is also helpful to add to research notes. Don't forget to write on the photocopies the author, title, date of publication and publisher of the book and the name of the library and the date when photocopied; or photocopy the title page and add any of the above information that is not on it. All notes, notebooks, and other personal research materials should contain the name and address of the researcher. A return address sticker is a quick way to handle this. Librarians discard reams of lost notes and notebooks annually because there is no identification on the material (see also "Lost and Found" in the next chapter).

SPECIAL COLLECTIONS ROOM

Nearly all of the materials in the Special Collections Room relate to LDS temple records, including the *Temple Records Index Bureau.* They are limited to use by LDS members who have either a temple recommend or a bishop's recommend for their use. There are a few other non-LDS collections housed therein that have special use requirements, such as close relationships. The Special Collections Room is located on the main floor.

TEMPLE RECORDS INDEX BUREAU

Another index that may be useful to have checked is the *Temple Records Index Bureau* (*TIB*). It contains approximately thirty million names for research done between 1927 and 1970. It is the predecessor of the *International Genealogical Index.* However, it is not as productive for researchers as the *IGI.* Researchers who have exhausted many other sources or who had ancestors who were members of the Church of Jesus Christ of Latter-days Saints should definitely consult this index for ancestors not found in the *IGI* or the *Family Group Records Collection.*

The *TIB* is an unpublished card file of the Family History Library and includes the names of individuals born between 1501 and 1970. It is international in scope and is arranged first by country of birth and subarranged in alphabetical order. The pamphlet listed under "Additional Reading" below provides details concerning its contents and use.

In order to protect the rights of privacy of the individuals listed in the *TIB* that are still living, it is not open for use by the general public. However, it may be consulted by mail for a small fee through the use of

a request form that is available from the Family History Library or at
its Family History Centers. The *TIB* may also be checked in the
Special Collections Room 124, main floor, by accredited genealogists
and active members of the LDS Church who have temple recommends
or letters of recommendation from their Bishop. Search requests are
limited to direct line ancestors of the researcher or client of an
accredited genealogist who has either a temple or bishop's recommend.

The name and address of the person who submitted the data is not
provided on the *TIB*, and for many cards, the information on the *TIB*
card is taken from the *Family Group Records Collection* form. The
information on the *TIB* will eventually be available on *FamilySearch*.

I. FAMILY HISTORY CENTER USERS:

If you have already used the *Family History Library Catalog* in a
Family History Center, upon arrival at your floor of research interest,
take out your prioritized bibliographic cards and find the first item in
the collection.

II. LOCAL PUBLIC LIBRARY USERS:

Find the floor on which your books, microfilm, and microfiche will be
located and select a microfiche reader that is located next to the *Family
History Library Catalog* or a *FamilySearch* computer station. Select the
microfiche or search the *FamilySearch* for the state and county or
family name on your prioritized bibliographic cards and look up the
Family History Library call number for your first item, following the
directions for use of the *Family History Library Catalog* in chapters 5
and 6.

You should also consult the *Family History Library Catalog* for your
geographical, individual or family surname cards and look up the call
numbers for the research materials needed.

Chapter 11

III. HOME LIBRARY USERS:

Find the floor on which the materials for your country of interest are located and select a microfiche reader by the *Family History Library Catalog* or a *FamilySearch* computer station. Follow the directions for use of the *Family History Library Catalog* in chapter 6. Find the microfiche for the state and county or family name of your prioritized research cards and look for materials that may be of use in your research.

Please remember to read the locality part of the *Catalog* on microfiche and/or on *FamilySearch* backwards, starting with the "Vital Records" of city, county, or state and moving towards the front of the catalog through "Probate Records," "Land Records," "Church Records," "Census Records," and "Biography." Following this backwards reading method, the records are arranged generally in order of importance. It is more economical to use the microfilmed vital records of a county that may be available in the Family History Library rather than writing for and paying for individual certificates.

SUMMARY:

All research is time-consuming. However, adequate preparation can make your research time in Salt Lake more efficient, enjoyable, and productive.

"Do yourself a favor and go to Salt Lake City and use these records."

-- An archives clerk at the Scottish Records Office to a Modesto, California researcher using parish registers on microfilm, filmed by the Family History Library

Chapter 12

MISCELLANEOUS SERVICES AT THE FAMILY HISTORY LIBRARY

BULLETIN BOARDS

There is a bulletin board at the Library entrance which lists classes being offered. Additional bulletin boards on each floor also list classes, as well as announcements and floor plans.

CHANGE MACHINES

All photocopy machines and vending machines make change for quarters and dimes and some for U.S. dollar bills. Please do not use any foreign coins in them (including Canadian coins; they jam the machines). There are bill changers in the Copy Centers and in the Snack Room. Also the Library Attendants' Stations adjacent to the Copy Centers have some change for larger bills.

COMPUTERS

Most of the computers contain *FamilySearch* and its files: *Ancestral File, International Genealogical Index, Personal Ancestral File, Social Security Death Index, Military Index* and portions of the *Family History Library Catalog*. In order to use a computer more than a few minutes you need to sign up for those that may be used for an hour at a time.

There are some computers that contain the *Personal Ancestral File*. If you plan to use these *PAF* computers or download to diskettes from *FamilySearch* files, you need to supply your own formatted diskettes or you can buy pre-formatted 5¼" and 3½" diskettes at the Library Attendants' Stations.

Chapter 12

COPY MACHINES

Copy Centers with photocopy machines for books, microfilm, and microfiche are located on the east side of each floor (to your left as you enter the reading room of each floor). Typewriters, paper cutters, staplers, pencils, genealogical supplies, hole punches, and bill change machines are also available in or near the Copy Centers.

DIRECTORIES

Building directories are located between the two main elevators on each floor, inside the entrance to each floor's reference area, and in each elevator.

FAMILYSEARCH CENTER

The *FamilySearch* Center will open in the historic Hotel Utah, South Temple and Main Streets in late summer 1993 and provide orientation films, books, microforms, and computers containing the *FamilySearch* program for beginning researchers .

FOOD

Patrons are requested not to bring food and drinks into areas of the Library outside of the Snack Room. See the paragraph under the heading "Snack Room" in this chapter and the list of eating places in the first part of chapter 13. The Snack Room is on the main floor, room 132.

FOREIGN LANGUAGE TRANSLATION

Brief translation assistance is usually available for some foreign languages as time and staff are available at reference desks in the foreign language departments of the Library. Also, there are word lists

available for purchase at the Library Attendants' Stations on the
foreign research floors.

GIFTS

The Library welcomes your gifts of manuscripts and printed records of
or about your family. The Acquisitions Unit of the Library is on the
third floor of the Library. Please call their office to arrange to present
your gift in person or by mail, (801) 240-2337. Your gift will be more
useful to other researchers if you also give the Library written
permission to microfilm your gift for world-wide use through the
Library's Family History Centers.

GROUP USE OF THE LIBRARY

Groups of ten or more researchers are requested to register in advance
to use the Library by writing the Family History Library, 35 North
West Temple Street, Salt Lake City, UT 84150, or by telephoning
(801) 240-2331. Advance registration helps the Library staff better
prepare to help researchers during a group visit.

HOLIDAYS

The Library is closed on the following days or the legal holiday, if the
normal holiday falls on a Sunday:
>   New Year's Eve at 5:00 p.m.
>   New Year's Day
>   Memorial Day
>   4th of July
>   24th of July, Pioneer Day, a Utah State holiday
>   Labor Day
>   Thanksgiving Day
>   The day before Christmas
>   Christmas Day

Chapter 12

On rare occasions, a severe winter storm or power outage will cause the Family History Library to close early. If you are in Salt Lake City for research and are, unfortunately, faced with this problem, you could spend the hours profitably by reviewing your research problems, objectives, and notes. However, another comprehensive collection that could be used on power outage days is the genealogical collection at the Utah Valley Regional Family History Center at the Harold B. Lee Library of Brigham Young University, Provo, Utah. Provo is forty-four miles south of Salt Lake City and is accessible via inexpensive public bus transportation. The Wilkinson Center next to and east of the Library has a fast food center (CougarEat), a cafeteria, and Skyroom Restaurant (top floor with a fine view). The author's favorite off-campus eatery is the Brick Oven, 200 East and 700 North (801) 374-8800 with homemade pasta and the West's best root beer.

HOURS

The hours of the Family History Library are as follows:

Monday	7:30 a.m. to 6:00 p.m.
Tuesday through Friday	7:30 a.m. to 10:00 p.m.
Saturday	7:30 a.m. to 5:00 p.m.

INFORMATION DESK

The desk in the main entrance lobby is an information desk, not a Library reference desk. The volunteers there will assist you with directions to the different facilities of the Library, research floors, and city sights and services.

INSTRUCTIONAL LECTURES

The Library offers lectures or classes in family history research and use of the Family History Library, including the use of some of its most important research resources. Lectures cover a great variety of subjects on how-to-do research, the major research tools in the Library,

FamilySearch and its parts, and the *Personal Ancestral File*. A free copy of the schedule of lectures may be obtained by writing the Family History Library, 35 North West Temple Street, Salt Lake City, UT 84150 or by telephoning (801) 240-2331. Lectures are held in classrooms B214 on the basement 2d floor; 134 and 136 on the main floor; and 218 on the second floor.

LOCKERS

Locker are available for day use only on all floors, near the Copy Centers.

LOST AND FOUND

Lost materials are taken by the staff to the Copy Center (room 112) on the main floor. The Library keeps lost items for eight weeks and does not accept responsibility for lost items.

MESSAGES AND MAIL

Have mail sent to the hotel or motel where you are planning to stay. Please do not have people call or send mail for you to the Library. There is a message board in the main floor lobby to aid you in contacting others in the Library. Paging patrons via the Library loudspeakers is available only for "life and death" matters and must be approved by Library security.

ORIENTATION

The Information Desk is opposite the entrance; to its left is an Orientation Center where you can see a film explaining how to do family history research and how to use the Library. You will also find out why Latter-day Saints do genealogical research and what they do in their temples. Two theaters, rooms 108 and 110, are part of the

Chapter 12

Orientation Center. The film presentations are 15 minutes in length and start about every 10 minutes, followed by a brief talk at the viewing window about how to use a couple of basic research tools. A how-to-use-it Library guide can be purchased at that time. It is also on sale at the Copy Centers on each floor. The Orientation Center will be moved to the *FamilySearch* Center in the historic Hotel Utah, South Temple and Main Streets in late summer 1993.

REFERENCE BOOKS

The Library's most often used reference tools are shelved near the Information Desk on each floor. Be sure to browse them for works of interest.

RESEARCHERS FOR HIRE

If you want to hire a professional genealogist to help you, ask at any Information Desk for a list of Accredited Researchers. You may also wish to consult the following additional list of professional genealogists:

Roster of Persons Certified as of November 1989. Washington, D.C.: Board for Certification of Genealogists, (P.O. Box 19165, Washington, DC 20036-0165) 1989.
    FHL U.S. & CAN REF AREA 973 A1 no. 209.

"Directory of Professional Genealogical Researchers." *Genealogical Helper*, September-October issue of each year.
    FHL GENERAL BOOK AREA 929.05 G286

Directory of Professional Genealogists. Salt Lake City: Association of Professional Genealogists, 1990.
    FHL GENERAL REF AREA 929.1 D628 1990.

Additional professional genealogists are listed in the telephone yellow pages under the subject heading, "Genealogists." A recent edition of the US West Communications Yellow Pages for Salt Lake City contained twenty entries.

There are many professional genealogists doing research daily in the Library. Observe the genealogists to see who, by their methods of research, appear to be the most knowledgeable. Ask them if they are acquainted with professional genealogists, and you may be able to make direct contact right in the Library. However, they are restricted by Library policy from soliciting.

RESTROOMS

Restrooms are located on the north side of each floor (to your right as you enter the reading room of each floor).

SECURITY

There is a security control at the door to check all briefcases, bags, and purses of exiting researchers. A plainclothes security officer is usually in the lobby of the main floor. You should keep your valuables with you at all times. Some women find small purses with shoulder straps or waist packs are useful for keeping their change and keys. Lockers are available for day use only on all floors, near the Copy Centers, for items that you do not need with you for research. The Library will not accept responsibility for items stolen or lost.

SMOKING

Smokers are asked not to smoke in the Library, the restrooms, or on the premises, which includes the planter box ledges in front of the Library. You may see some people who smoke while resting on the front planter boxes. They show a discourtesy to the Church that provides them free access to the world's largest genealogical library.

SNACK ROOM

A Snack Room is available on the north end of the main floor (to the left of the rest rooms) for eating bag lunches brought into the Library. A microwave oven, straws, and paper napkins are provided free of charge. Vending machines include choices of cold soft drinks, milk, juice, sandwiches, bagels, hot dogs, corn dogs, burritos, pizzas, salads, apples, chips, cookies, donuts, cakes, fruit pies, yogurt, ice cream bars, ice cream sandwiches, and candies. A bill change machine is available in the Snack Room (Room 132).

SPECIAL NEEDS PATRON SERVICES

Wheelchair access entrance doors and microfilm readers are available and some assistance for the hearing-impaired is provided. Wheelchairs are available for Library use by request at the lobby Information Desk. A Visualtak reader (for books) is available on the main floor for sight-impaired. Telephone (801) 240-4428 concerning details of Special Needs Patron Services.

STAMPS

A full value Postal Products machine is located by the elevators on the Main Floor. A mail box is near the crosswalk in front of the Library. A post office substation is three blocks from the Library at 230 West 200 South Street.

SUPPLIES

Some researchers have found that printed research forms are time-saving and efficient. Forms for recording data from the U.S. federal census schedules are helpful, as are Research Logs. These forms and others, along with research papers, are available for sale in the Copy Centers. Pencils, pens, envelopes, pre-formatted computer diskettes, and scratch paper are also available for sale. Forms which pertain to geographical areas are available only on the floors relating to their research. The nearest stationary store is Quick Connection in the Crossroads Mall on the lower level in the South hall (328-1099).

Additional supplies, as well as genealogical books, are available at the following nearby businesses:

Heritage Quest Genealogy Resource Center, 122 West Temple Street, next door to the Library in the Howard Johnson Hotel Lobby; turn left at the front desk. The Center is near the end of the hall and on the right hand side (801) 359-9353.

Everton Publishers, Inc., 165 South West Temple Street, #200, directly across from the main entrance to the Salt Palace. Hours: 10:00 a.m. to 4:00 p.m., Monday through Friday, (801) 521-2389.

Deseret Book in the ZCMI Center (mall) right behind the Park Food Court at the South Temple entrance (Number 13 on the attractions map on the inside back cover of this work). The genealogy section is in the back of the store.

TELEPHONES

There are telephones near the elevators on each floor. Local calls are twenty-five cents.

Family History Library telephone numbers:
(Gifts) Book Acquisitions	(801) 240-2337
Information Desks	
Asian (Catalog Dept.)	(801) 240-1372
British	(801) 240-2367
European	(801) 240-2881
General	(801) 240-2331
Latter-day Saint	(801) 240-2720
Scandinavian	(801) 240-2198
Spanish	(801) 240-1738
U.S.-Canadian (Books)	(801) 240-2720
U.S.-Canadian (Microform)	(801) 240-2364

Chapter 12

TYPEWRITERS

Free typewriters are available in Copy Centers.

SUMMARY:

The Library may appear somewhat overwhelming. However, it is really not too complicated, and the staff and volunteers are very helpful. Try to find things yourself, but don't hesitate to ask for assistance at the Information Desk or Library Attendants' Stations when you can't do it on your own. Work hard and enjoy your research at the world's largest genealogical library.

Shortly after the festive wedding of Prince Charles to Diana, a lady came into the Family History Center and declared that she wanted to prove her relationship to the Queen of England because: "My niece looks just like the Queen Mother, and my family descends from Prince George who came over on the Mayflower."

-- Modesto California Family History Center, 1981

MAIN FLOOR PLAN: UNITED STATES AND CANADA
INFORMATION AND BOOKS

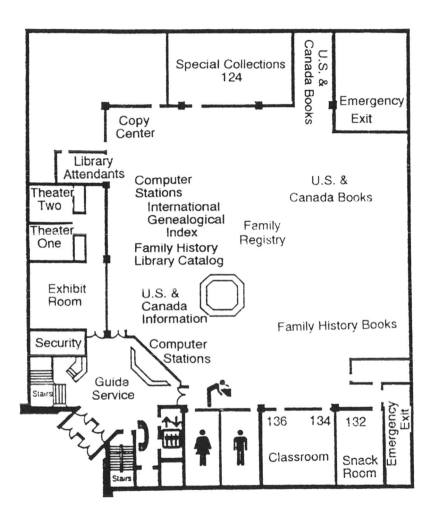

SECOND FLOOR PLAN: UNITED STATES AND CANADA
MICROFORMS

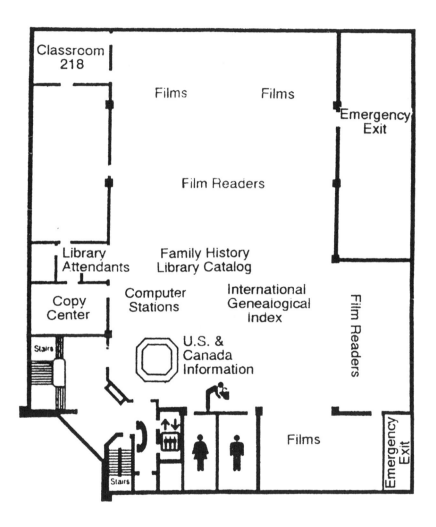

BASEMENT 1 FLOOR PLAN: EUROPE, SCANDINAVIA, LATIN AMERICA, AND INTERNATIONAL

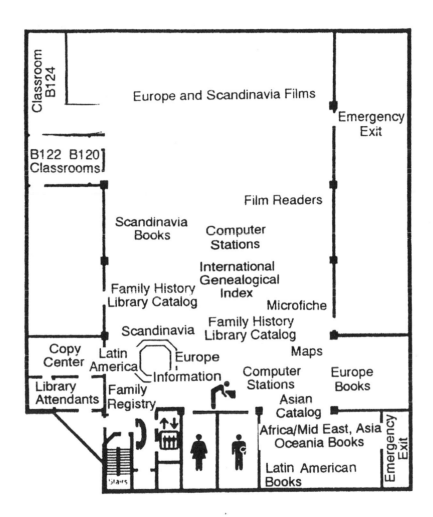

BASEMENT 2 FLOOR PLAN: BRITISH ISLES

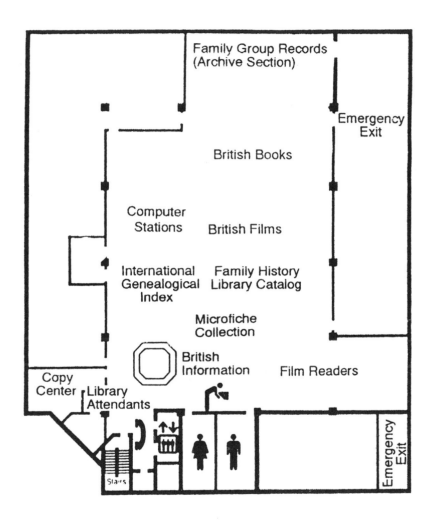

Chapter 13

DINING, LODGING, AND HEALTH CARE IN SALT LAKE CITY

The Family History Library Snack Room on the north end to the left of the restrooms on the main floor has been explained in chapter 12, under "Snack Room". Following is a list of nearby restaurants and fast food eateries:

RESTAURANTS AND FAST FOOD ESTABLISHMENTS NOT AFFILIATED WITH HOTELS (Listed in order of proximity to the Library):

JB's Restaurant, on the corner of South Temple and West Temple, next to the Library, 122 West South Temple Street, (801) 328-8344.

Carriage Court Restaurant in The Inn at Temple Square, 75 West South Temple Street, 84101, (801) 536-7200. One dining critic has praised it as having better cuisine than a cruise ship.

Snelgrove Ice Cream Soup & Sandwiches, 65 West South Temple Street, (801) 534-0246.

JB's Restaurant, Crossroads Plaza Mall across from McDonald's, (801) 355-2100. The Crossroads Plaza Mall is shown as number 15 on the attractions map on the inside back cover of this work.

McDonald's, 50 West South Temple Street, at the entrance to the Crossroads Plaza Mall, (801) 322-0362.

There are several fast food stands in the "Richards Street Marketplace" in the basement of the Crossroads Plaza Mall.

Dee's Family Restaurant, 143 West North Temple Street, (801) 359-4414.

Chapter 13

When the Hotel Utah (located on the northeast corner of South Temple Street and Main Street, and number 8 on the attractions map on the inside back cover of this work) renovation project is finished, the restaurant reestablished on the top (tenth) floor will again offer some good views of the city, Temple Square, and sunsets. The new names of both the building and restaurant are yet to be determined and the projected completion date is late summer of 1993.

The Park Food Court in the ZCMI Center on the south side of South Temple east of Main Street. A Burger King and other fast food stands are located in the Park Food Court. The ZCMI Center is shown as number 14 on the attractions map on the inside back cover of this work.

Skool Lunch (deli and bakery), 60 East South Temple Street, #105, (801) 532-5269.

The Lion House (1855), 63 East South Temple Street, provides a membership fee cafeteria in its basement and permits the general public to buy lunch at a very small extra cost. It is worth the little extra walk. (801) 363-5466. Take the sidewalk along the West or left side of the House to the entrance near the back of the building (number 9 on the attractions map on the inside back cover of this work). National Registry of Historic Places, 1856.
> "...Johnson professed to have enjoyed a sociable breakfast in the Lion House. He gave a preposterous account of the 'calling of the roll,' and other preliminaries, and the carnage that ensued when the buckwheat-cakes came in. But he embellished rather too much."
> -- Mark Twain, *Roughing It* (New York: Grosset & Dunlap, 1913), page 70. Originally published : New York: American Publishing Co., 1871. Twain visited Salt Lake City in 1861.

Patrons of the Library are welcome to eat at the Cafeteria at The Church of Jesus Christ of Latter-day Saints Office Building, 50 East North Temple Street, hours 7:00 a.m. - 7:45 a.m.; 9:00 a.m. - 10:30 a.m.; and 11:30 a.m. - 1:45 p.m. A guest pass is required and may be obtained free at the Information Desk in the lobby on the Main Floor of the Library. No tea or coffee is served and smoking is not permitted. The Church Office Building is shown as number 6 on the attractions map on the inside back cover of this work.

136

Chart House Restaurant, 334 West South Temple Street, (801) 596-0990. Dinner only. In the Devereaux House near the Delta Center. The Devereaux House is on the National Registry of Historic Places, 1857, and is shown as number 30 on the attractions map on the inside back cover of this work.

IS UTAH WET OR DRY?

One of the readers of the first edition of *Going* suggested that something be included in the second edition about Utah's liquor laws:

LIQUOR LAWS
Utah's liquor laws are easy to understand. Alcoholic beverages are served with your meal in most restaurants and hotels. Liquor may be purchased in state liquor stores throughout Salt Lake. Mixed drinks are served in Utah's non-exclusive private clubs (visitors are welcome at these clubs, and temporary memberships are available for a nominal fee). The only difference between private clubs and public restaurants is the time of day the drinks may be served; private clubs may serve alcoholic drinks throughout the day and in restaurants, only after 1 p.m.

STATE LIQUOR STORES
State Liquor Stores sell packaged liquors and wines in various sized bottles. Utah also has several innovative "Wine Stores" that provide a wide variety and selection of wines from around the world. In all State Stores, you must pay cash; checks or credit cards are not accepted. State Liquor Stores are not open on Sundays and holidays.

Chapter 13

DRINKING AND DRIVING

Its not a good idea to drive under the influence of
alcohol anywhere; Utah is no exception. Utah laws,
similar to many Western states, are stringent. 0.08%
or more alcohol to blood content is considered drunk
and constitutes "Driving Under the Influence."
-- Salt Lake Convention & Visitors Bureau
Salt Lake Visitors Guide

NEAREST HOTELS AND MOTELS (Listed in order of proximity to
the Library):

Within one block of the Library (BEWARE! Visitors are
often surprised at the generous length of a Salt Lake
City block):

Howard Johnson, next door to the Library at 122 West South Temple
Street, 84101, (801) 521-0130 (800 366-3684 or 800 654-2000), FAX
(801) 322-5051. Has a JB's Big Boy Family Restaurant adjacent,
courtesy airport shuttle, and exercise room (number 4 on the
accommodations map on page 197 of this work).

The Inn at Temple Square, 71 West South Temple Street, 84101, (801)
531-1000, FAX (801) 536-7272. Totally Nonsmoking. One dining
critic has praised its elegant Carriage Court Restaurant as having better
cuisine than a cruise ship (number 6 on the accommodations map on
page 197 of this work).

Marriott Hotel, 75 South West Temple Street, 84101, (801) 531-0800
(800 228-9290). Courtesy airport shuttle, full breakfast on Friday and
Saturday, indoor pool, recreational program, weight room, exercise
room, tennis courts, and racquetball courts (number 9 on the
accommodations map on page 197 of this work).

Salt Lake TraveLodge at Temple Square, 144 West North Temple
Street, 84103, (801) 533-8200 (800 255-3050, number 1 on the
accommodations map on page 197 of this work).

Within two blocks of the Library:

Covered Wagon Motel, 230 West North Temple Street, 84103, (801) 533-9100.

Doubletree Hotel, 215 West Temple Street, 84101, (801) 531-7500 (800 528-0444). Courtesy airport shuttle, full breakfast, elegant restaurant on first floor, indoor pool, and exercise room (number 5 on the accommodations map on page 197 of this work).

The Kimball, 150 North Main Street, 84103, (801) 363-4000. A time share with some shares available for purchase. A Resort Condominiums International and Interval International Resort Directory participant. No overnight guests accommodated without membership or exchange (number 2 on the accommodations map on page 197 of this work).

Within three blocks of the Library:

Royal Executive Inn, 121 North 300 West Street, 84103, (801) 521-3450 (800 541-7639). Courtesy airport shuttle.

Carlton Hotel, 140 East South Temple Street, 84111, (801) 355-3418. Courtesy Family History Library and airport shuttle.

Shilo Inn, 206 South West Temple Street, 84101, (801) 521-9500 (800 222-2244). Restaurant and exercise room (number 9 on the accommodations map on page 197 of this work).

Peery Hotel, 110 West 300 South Street, 84101, (801) 521-4300 (Outside Utah 800 331-0073), FAX (801) 575-5014. Courtesy airport shuttle, continental breakfast, restaurants, and exercise room (number 11 on the accommodations map on page 197 of this work). National Registry of Historic Places, 1910.

Chapter 13

Red Lion Hotel, 255 South West Temple Street, 84101, (801) 328-2000 (800 547-8010). Courtesy airport shuttle, restaurants, indoor pool, and exercise room (number 10 on the accommodations map on page 197 of this work).

SELECTED ECONOMY MOTELS IN THE CITY AND AREA
(Listed in order of proximity to the Library):

Motel 6, 176 West 600 South Street, 84101, (801) 531-1252. Nationwide reservations (505) 891-6161.

Super 8 Motel, 616 South 200 West Street, 84101, (801) 534-0808 (800 843-1991) (number 22 on the accommodations map on page 197 of this work).

Emerald Inn, 476 South State Street, 84111, (801) 533-9300 (number 16 on the accommodations map on page 197 of this work).

Econo Lodge, 715 West North Temple Street, 84116, (801) 363-0062, FAX (801) 359-3926. Courtesy airport shuttle.

SELECTED NATIONAL CHAIN HOTELS AND MOTELS IN THE CITY AND AREA (Listed in order of proximity to the Library):

Deseret Inn, 50 West 500 South Street, 84101, (801) 532-8538. Restaurants (number 15 on the accommodations map on page 197 of this work).

Hilton Hotel, 150 West 500 South Street, 84101, (801) 532-3344 (800 445-8667). Courtesy airport shuttle, but the hotel asks that you tip the driver. Restaurants and exercise room (number 14 on the accommodations map on page 197 of this work).

Little America Hotel and Towers, 500 South Main Street, 84101, (801) 363-6781 (800 453-9450), FAX (801) 3323-1610. Courtesy airport shuttle, restaurants, indoor pool, and exercise room (number 18 on the accommodations map on page 197 of this work).

Salt Lake City Center TraveLodge, 524 South West Temple Street, 84101, (801) 531-7100 (800 255-3050), FAX (801) 359-3814 (number 17 on the accommodations map on page 197 of this work).

Quality Inn - City Center, 154 West 600 South Street, 84101, (801) 521-2930 (800 221-2222 or 800 424-6423). Courtesy airport shuttle, continental breakfast, and restaurants (number 20 on the accommodations map on page 197 of this work).

Best Western Olympus Hotel, 161 West 600 South Street, 84101, (801) 521-7373 (800 426-0722), FAX (801) 524-0354. Non-smoking floors. Courtesy shuttle to airport and to other downtown hotels, restaurant, and exercise room (number 23 on the accommodations map on page 197 of this work).

Embassy Suites Hotel, 600 South West Temple Street, 84065, (801) 359-7800 (800 362-2779). Courtesy airport shuttle, full breakfast, indoor pool, and exercise room (number 21 on the accommodations map on page 197 of this work).

Holiday Inn - Downtown, 230 West 600 South Street, 84101, (801) 532-7000 (800 465-4329). Courtesy airport shuttle, restaurant, and indoor pool (number 19 on the accommodations map on page 197 of this work).

Mountain City Suites, 352 South 300 East, 84111, (801) 521-3790 (800 765-8819). Restaurant (number 12 on the accommodations map on page 197 of this work).

Clarion Hotel & Suites, 999 South Main Street, 84111, (801) 359-8600 (800 933-9678). Courtesy shuttle to airport and to other downtown hotels, restaurant, pool enclosed in winter, tennis courts, and exercise room.

Residence Inn by Marriott, 765 East 400 South, 84102, (801) 532-5511 (800 228-9290). Courtesy airport shuttle, continental breakfast, and sports court (number 13 on the accommodations map on page 197 of this work).

Chapter 13

National 9 Inn, 1025 North 900 West Street, 84116, (801) 364 6591 (800 524-9999).

Holiday Inn Airport, 1659 West North Temple, 84116, (801) 533-9000 (800 465-4329). Courtesy airport shuttle. Restaurant.

Days Inn, 1900 West North Temple Street, 84116, (801) 539-8538 (800 325-2525). Courtesy airport shuttle and continental breakfast (5/15-10/15).

Motel 6, 1990 West Temple Street, 84116, (801) 364-1053. Nationwide reservations (505) 891-6161.

Nendels Inn Airport. 2080 West North Temple, 84116, (801) 355-0088 (800 626-2824 or 800 547-0106), FAX (801) 355-0099. Courtesy airport shuttle, continental breakfast, and restaurant next door.

Radisson Hotel-Salt Lake City Airport, 2177 West North Temple Street, 84116, (801) 364-5800 (800 333-3333), FAX 364-5823. Courtesy airport shuttle, full breakfast, restaurant, and exercise room.

Comfort Inn-Salt Lake City Airport, 200 North Admiral Byrd Road, 84116, (801) 537-7444 (800 535-8742 or 800 228-5150), FAX (801) 532-4721. Courtesy shuttle to airport and to other downtown hotels. Continental breakfast. Restaurant.

Quality Inn Airport and International Center, 5575 West Amelia Earhart Drive, 84116, (801) 537-7020 (800 522-5575 or 800 424-6423), FAX (801) 537-7020. Courtesy shuttle to airport and to other downtown hotels. Restaurant.

Airport Hilton, 5151 Wiley Post Way, 84116, (801) 539-1515 (800 999-3736), FAX (801) 539-1113. Courtesy airport shuttle, restaurant, indoor pool, sports court, and exercise room.

Motel 6, 2433 South 800 West Street, Woods Cross, 84087, (801) 298-0289. Nationwide reservations (505) 891-6161.

Motel 6, 496 Catalpa Drive, Midvale, 84047, (801) 561-0058.
Nationwide reservations 505 891-6161.

La Quinta Motor Inn, 530 Catalpa Road, Midvale, 84047, (801) 566-3291 (800 531-5900), FAX (801) 562-5943. Courtesy airport shuttle.

Comfort Inn, 8955 South 255 West Street, Sandy, 84070, (12 miles south) (801) 255-4919 (800 228-5150), FAX (801) 255-4998.
Continental breakfast and indoor pool.

BED AND BREAKFASTS (Listed in order of proximity to the Library):

Anton Boxrud Bed & Breakfast, 57 South 600 East Street, 84102, (801) 363-8035. National Registry of Historic Places, 1900. Full breakfast, and no smoking indoors (number 7 on the accommodations map on page 197 of this work).

Saltair Bed & Breakfast, 164 South 900 East Street, 84102, (801) 533-8184. National Registry of Historic Places. Full breakfast and totally non-smoking.

Brigham Street Inn, 1135 East South Temple Street, 84102, (801) 364-4461. National Registry of Historic Places, 1898. Continental breakfast.

Pinecrest Bed and Breakfast Inn, 6211 Emigration Canyon Road, 84108, (801) 583-6663. National Registry of Historic Places, 1915.
Continental breakfast and no smoking indoors.

CONDOMINIUMS (Listed in order of proximity to the Library):

The Kimball, 150 North Main Street, 84103, (801) 363-4000. A time share with some shares available for purchase. A Resort Condominiums International (RCI) and Interval International Resort Directory (II) participant. No overnight guests accommodated without membership or exchange (number 2 on the accommodations map on page 197 of this work). Within two blocks of the Library.

Circle J Club at Jeremy Ranch, 4065 Jeremy Woods Road, Park City, 84060, (801) 649-0370, 25 miles from the Library, an RCI participant. Park City is at an elevation of 6,911 compared to Salt Lake City's 4,390 feet.

Iron Blosam Lodge-Snowbird, Snowbird, 84092, (801) 742-2222, 26 miles from the Library, an RCI and II participant. Snowbird is at an elevation of 8,100 feet, rising nearly 3,500 feet in the last eight miles.

Park Avenue Condominiums, 1650 Park Avenue, Park City, 84060, (801) 649-4500, 30 miles from the Library, an RCI participant.

Park Hotel Condominiums, 605 Main Street, Park City, 84060, (801) 649-3200, 35 miles from the Library, an RCI participant.

Park Plaza, 2060 Sidewinder Drive, Park City, 84060, (801) 649-0870, 35 miles from the Library, an RCI and II participant.

Park Regency Utah, 1710 Prospector Road, Park City, 84060, (801) 645-7531, 35 miles from the Library, an RCI and II participant.

Sweetwater at Park City, 1255 Empire Avenue, Park City, 84060, (801) 649-9651, 35 miles from the Library, an RCI participant.

Wolf Creek Village, 3900 North Wolf Creek Drive, Eden, 84310, (801) 745-0222, 52 miles from the Library, an RCI participant.

HOSTELS (Listed in order of proximity to the Library):

The Avenue's Residential Center, 107 F Street, 84103, (801) 363-8137 (6 blocks east of the Library). Member of AYH (number 3 on the accommodations map on page 197 of this work).

AAIH Kendel Hostel & Motel, 667 North 300 West Street, (801) 355-0293.

CAMPING (Listed in order of proximity to the Library):

Campground V.I.P., 1350 West North Temple Street, 84116, (801) 328-0224.

KOA (AAA), 1400 West North Temple Street, 84116, (801) 355-1192.

Mountain Shadows RV Park, 13275 South Minuteman Drive, Draper, (801) 571-4024, 16 miles from the Library.

Pioneer Village Campground, 135 North Lagoon Drive, Farmington, 84025, (801) 451-2812, 17 miles from the Library (Lagoon amusement park admission and swimming included - take Lagoon exit).

Cherry Hill Camping Resort, 1325 South Main Street, Kaysville, 84037, (801) 451-5379, 19 miles from the Library (may be the quietest location of the commercial campgrounds).

Wasatch National Forest campsites (without showers) in Big Cottonwood Canyon (SR-152), 19 miles from the Library and Little Cottonwood Canyon (SR-210) southeast of the city, 23 miles from the Library.

Hidden Haven Campground, east of the city on I-80, 2200 West Rasmussen Road, Park City, 84060, (801) 649-8935, 35 miles from the Library.

There are also other beautiful campsites (without showers) in the Wasatch National Forest; however, most of them are quite distant from the Library.

HEALTH CARE

Unfortunately, researchers sometimes need medical attention while traveling. Salt Lake City has some of the West's best health care facilities and physicians. However, the following medical facilities and professionals are listed because of their locations, without any personal recommendation of the author.

145

Chapter 13

Hospitals (Listed in order of proximity to the Library):

Holy Cross Hospital, 1050 East South Temple Street, 84102, (801) 350-4111; 24-Hour Emergency 350-4631; Physician Referral 350-4288.

LDS Hospital, 8th Avenue & C Street, (801) 321-1100; 24-Hour Emergency 321-1180.

University Hospital & Clinics, 50 North Medical Drive, 84132, (801) 581-2121; 24-Hour Emergency 581-2291; Physician Referral (801) 581-2897 (800 662-0052).

Physicians - Family Practice (Listed in order of proximity to the Library):

Dr. Roslyn Taylor, 1002 East South Temple Street, (801) 350-4461.

Dr. John M. Tudor, Jr., 1060 East 100 South Street, (801) 531-8634.

Dr. J. Darrell Thueson, Salt Lake Clinic, 333 South 900 East Street, (801) 535-8398.

Utah Medical Association, State-wide referral, (801) 355-7477.

ASK-A-NURSE, free 24-hour health care hotline staffed by registered nurses, (801) 972-8488.

Dentists (Listed in order of proximity to the Library):

Dr. Donald A. Brooks, 10 East South Temple Street, (801) 364-7943.

Dr. F. Richard Austin, 60 East South Temple, Suite 610, (801) 321-7600.

Dr. Bengt J. Jonsson, 370 East South Temple Street, (801) 328-3169.

Dr. Mark James Callan, 370 East South Temple Street, Suite 220, (801) 355-8287.

(800) - DENTIST (336-8478).

Chiropractic Physicians (Listed in order of proximity to the Library):

Accident Chiropractic, 418 East 300 South Street, (801) 363-7000. 24 hour emergency care.

Dr. Richard K. Madsen, 337 South 400 East Street, (801) 521-0800.

Dr. Joseph Nicolich, Avenues Chiropractic Center, 382 4th Avenue, (801) 355-2024.

Dr. Orson P. Kesler, Midvale Chiropractic Office, Locust and Center, Midvale, 84047, (801) 255-3871.
An excellent chiropractor; ask his secretary for directions to his office. Recommended by a Salt Lake City resident, friend of the author.

Utah Association of Chiropractic Physicians, Doctor Referral Hot Line, (801) 486-3747 (800 456-3820).

ADDITIONAL READING:

Salt Lake Restaurant Guide. Salt Lake City: Salt Lake Valley Convention & Visitors Bureau, 1989. Free. 180 South West Temple, Salt Lake City, Utah 84101-1493, (801) 521-2822.

American Automobile Association's *Colorado/Utah.* Heathrow, Fla.: American Automobile Association, 1991.

Chapter 13

SUMMARY:

Please eat three square meals a day. You'll need all the energy you can get. Make sure that you get enough sleep to have a good, clear head on your shoulders for doing research.

"Salt Lake City was healthy--an extremely healthy city. They declared that there was only one physician in the place and he was arrested every week regularly and held to answer under the vagrant act for having 'no visible means of support.'"
-- Mark Twain, *Roughing It* (New York: Grosset & Dunlap, 1913), page 64. Originally published: New York: American Publishing Co., 1871.
Twain visited Salt Lake City in 1861.

Chapter 14

TRANSPORTATION AND PARKING

BUSES

Greyhound Bus Lines, 160 West Temple Street, 84101, (801) 355-4684. The bus depot is just around the corner from the Library.

Local buses are operated by the Utah Transit Authority, 3600 South 700 West Street, 84119, (801) 287-4636.

AIRLINES

Many major airlines have routes to or through Salt Lake City. Airlines and their reservations telephone numbers for Salt Lake City are as follows:

America West	800 247-5692, (801) 328-0121
American	800 433-7300
Continental	(801) 359-9800
Delta	800 221-1212, (801) 532-7123
Horizon	800 547-9308
Northwest	800 225-2525
Skywest/Delta Connection	800-453-9417
TWA	(801) 539-1111
United	800 241-6522

Morris Travel provides some economy fare flights from major cities in the United States listed below; 260 East Morris Avenue, Salt Lake City, Utah 84415, (801) 483-6464 (800 444-5660).

Anchorage	Los Angeles	Phoenix	San Jose
Boise	Oakland	Portland	Seattle
Hawaii	Orange Co., CA	Sacramento	Spokane
Las Vegas	Orlando	San Diego	Twin Falls

149

Chapter 14

AIRPORT TRANSPORTATION

From the airport the Utah Transit Authority bus #50 runs:

Monday - Friday	6:31 a.m. - 11:48 p.m.	(26 trips)
Saturday	6:35 a.m. - 11:48 p.m.	(18 trips)
Sunday	6:34 a.m. - 5:34 p.m.	(5 trips)

To the airport bus #50 leaves the East side of Temple Square:

Monday - Friday	5:59 a.m. - 11:19 p.m.	(26 trips)
Saturday	6:04 a.m. - 11:19 p.m.	(18 trips)
Sunday	6:04 a.m. - 5:04 p.m.	(5 trips)

The airport is four miles west of the Library. For the latest stop locations and schedules, call Utah Transit Authority, (801) 287-4636.

RAILROADS

Amtrak, 81 North 400 West Street, (801) 364-8562 (800 872-7245). Very early morning arrival and late night departure. Amtrak is shown as number 31 on the attractions map on the inside back cover of this work.

TAXICABS

City Cab (801) 363-5014.

Ute Cab (801) 359-7788.

Yellow Cab (801) 521-2100.

PARKING (Listed in order of proximity to the Library):

There is a parking lot with a three-hour limit on the northwest corner of West Temple Street and North Temple Street; free with token from the Library during working hours. Exit can also be managed with $3.50 in quarters. No recreational vehicles or trailers permitted.

E-Z Auto Park, 30 West North Temple Street, (801) 322-2169. $3.00 for 0 - 12 hours. No recreational vehicles or trailers permitted nor in-and-outs.

The Main Street Parking, 132 North Main, on the northeast corner of Main Street and North Temple Street permits the parking of recreational vehicles or trailers, (801) 328-1244, $2.00 for all day.

Allright Parking, 2d West Street behind the Library, (801) 359-1152, $1.50 for all day. Coins needed.

The Parking Place, 240 West South Temple Street, a very large lot on the corner of 2d West Street and South Temple Street. $2.00 for all day; recreational vehicles or trailers are welcome.

Free all-day street parking is available within three blocks northwest of the Library, on 3rd North and West Temple and beyond.

AUTOMOBILE RENTING - DOWNTOWN LOCATIONS (Listed in order of proximity to the Library):

Hertz, Marriott Hotel, 75 South West Temple Street, 84101, (801) 355-8427; Red Lion Hotel, 255 South West Temple Street, 84101, (801) 328-8915 (800 654-3131).

Agency Rent-A-Car, 307 West 200 South Street, 84101, (801) 484-0320, (800 321-1972).

General Rent-A-Car, Salt Lake Hilton, 150 West 500 South Street, 84101, (801) 322-3941, (800 327-7607).

Chapter 14

Avis Rent A Car, Embassy Suite Hotel, 600 South West Temple Street, 84101, (801) 359-2177, (800 331-1212).

A Ute Rent-A-Car, 456 West 200 South Street, 84101, (801) 328-5709.

Budget & Sears, 750 South Main Street, 84101, (801) 322-5581, (800 527-0700).

Rent-A-Wreck, 741 South State Street, 84111, (801) 359-9900 (800 594-8976).

Thrifty Car Rental, 958 South State Street, 84111, (801) 355-7368, (800 367-2277).

SUMMARY:

Make sure that your travel plans include enough sleep in order to arrive in Salt Lake City rested and with enough energy to fly into sound research.

> "The city lies in the edge of a level plain as broad as the
> state of Connecticut, and crouches close down to the
> ground under a curving wall of mighty mountains whose
> heads are hidden in the clouds, and whose shoulders
> bear relics of the snows of winter all the summer long.
> Seen from one of these dizzy heights, twelve or fifteen
> miles off, Great Salt Lake City is toned down and
> diminished till it is suggestive of a child's toy village
> reposing under the majestic protection of the Chinese
> wall."
>   -- Mark Twain, *Roughing It* (New York: Grosset
>   & Dunlap, 1913), page 63. Originally published:
>   New York: American Publishing Co., 1871.
>   Twain visited Salt Lake City in 1861.

Chapter 15

SIGHTSEEING AND ENTERTAINMENT

Most researchers are reluctant to take time from their precious research at the Family History Library for sightseeing, shopping, or sporting.

For those who need a break or who have a family along that needs entertaining, the Salt Lake Convention & Visitors Bureau publishes an excellent free *Salt Lake Visitors Guide*. Pick one up upon arrival in Salt Lake City at Terminal 2 at the airport or at their South West Temple Street office, or write or call for one beforehand. The Bureau's address is 180 South West Temple Street, Salt Lake City, Utah 84101-1493, phone (801) 521-2822 (number 1 on the attractions map on the inside back cover of this work).

Various additional guides to events, tours, and sights, etc., are available from:

Utah Travel Council, Council Hall/Capitol Hill, Salt Lake City, UT 84114. (801) 538-1030. Their best publication is the *Tour Guide to Utah*.

Salt Lake Area Chamber of Commerce, 175 East 400 South Street, Salt Lake City, UT 84101. (801) 364-3631.

There are, of course, other guides to Utah's recreation. The American Automobile Association's *Colorado/Utah* is a very practical guide to historic sites, hotels, motels, and restaurants. Another is Bill Weir's *Utah Handbook*, 2d ed., (Chico, Calif.: Moon Publications, 1991, 722 Wall Street, 95928, (800) 345-5473, $12.95 paper, 452 pages).

SIGHTS

The following are the author's favorite sights:

Temple Square, 240-2534, across West Temple Street from the Library (number 5 on the attractions map on the inside back cover of this work). National Registry of Historic Places, 1855.

The Museum of Church History and Art, next door to the Library (number 4 on the attractions map on the inside back cover of this work), 240-3310.

The Tabernacle Choir's 9:15 a.m. Sunday morning CBS broadcast (usually no seats are available for tourists for the broadcast that precedes the Church's General Conference the first Sunday of April and October).

Trolley Square at 6th South and 9th East, (801) 521-9877. A fee trolley to the Square stops in front of the Library and a schedule is posted at its stop (number 34 on the attractions map on the inside back cover of this work).

The Tracy Aviary in Liberty Park at 859 East 1300 South. Admission charge.

The Alpine Scenic Loop, a spectacular seventy-four mile round trip drive from downtown Salt Lake City, climbing to an altitude of over 9,000 feet behind 11,750 Mt. Timpanogos and descending through American Fork Canyon back to the 4,500 elevation of Utah Valley. Take I-15 south of the city to Utah SR-52 (8th North Street in Orem). Take SR-52 east up Provo Canyon on Highway 189 to SR-92 and follow the signs back to I-15. Summer only.

Sunset over the Great Salt Lake from the foothills of Bountiful; take I-15 north of town and turn off on Bountiful's 5th South off ramp. Drive high up the hill, park, and drink in a glorious Utah treat. A shorter drive, but not as nice as Bountiful, is up North Main Street toward the State Capitol and right on either 3rd or 5th North Street to East Capitol Boulevard; then left (or up) the hill to Edgecombe Drive. Make a U-turn at Edgecombe Drive and return to the open area down the hill where you should find a good view. If not, drive back down to 7th North, turn right and look for a place to park with a good view on Cortez Street.

If you want to get into the Tabernacle, take the free guided tour or attend a concert, an organ recital, or the free Tabernacle Choir broadcast on Sunday from 9:15-10:00 a.m. or the Choir rehearsal on Thursday night, 8:00-9:30 p.m. Organ recitals are presented free Monday through Saturday, 12:00-12:30 p.m. and Sunday, 2:00 p.m. During the months of June through September additional organ recitals are presented Monday through Friday, 4:00-4:30 p.m. The Tabernacle is on the National Registry of Historic Places, 1862-1867.

There are free concerts in the Tabernacle and also in the air-conditioned Assembly Hall on the southwest corner of the Square. Ask for schedules at any of the visitor center desks or write Temple Square Visitor's Center, 50 North Temple Street, Salt Lake City UT 84050 or call (801) 240-4872. Persons who depend on air conditioning should be aware that the Tabernacle is not air conditioned and can be hot on some days and for some occasions.

Non-denominational Sunday services are also presented by the Church of Jesus Christ of Latter-day Saints in the Assembly Hall most Sunday mornings following the Tabernacle Choir broadcast.

"This is the Place" Monument in the Pioneer Trail State Park at the mouth of Emigration Canyon offers some historical background to the settlement of the Great Salt Lake Valley, as well as a fine view. Take South Temple Street east to 1300 East Street, turn right to 500 South Street, then left and east. 500 South Street becomes Foothill Drive. Turn left and east on Sunnyside Avenue to the park.

Kennecott's Bingham Canyon Mine, (801) 569-6000, is one of the largest open pit mines in the world and an interesting place to visit in summer. Take I-15 south to exit 301, then west to SR-48. The mine is at the end of SR-48, twenty-three miles southwest of the City. A small fee is charged for autos. National Registry of Historic Places, 1904.

SIGHTSEEING TOURS

Gray Line Motor Tours, 553 West 100 South Street, 84101, (801) 521-7060. City tours and tours of national parks.

155

Old Salty Tour Train, 549 West 500 South Street, 84101, (801) 359-8677. City lecture-tours in an open-air, rubber tire vehicle, three times a day from the Temple Square South gate, 11:00 a.m., 1:00 p.m., and 3:00 p.m..

CULTURE AND EDUCATION (Listed in order of proximity to the Library):

Symphony Hall, home of the Utah Symphony, 123 West South Temple Street, 84111, (801) 533-5626 (number 2 on the attractions map on the inside back cover of this work).

Salt Lake Art Center, 20 South West Temple, (801) 328-4201 (number 2 on the attractions map on the inside back cover of this work).

LDS Church Office Building, 50 East North Temple Street, 240-3789 provides a very high-rise view of the city from the top floor (number 6 on the attractions map on the inside back cover of this work).

Capitol Theatre, home of the Utah Opera Company, (801) 534-0888; and Ballet West, (801) 363-9318; 50 West 200 South Street, 84101 (number 17 on the attractions map on the inside back cover of this work).

Hansen Planetarium, 15 South State Street, (801) 538-2098 (Number 12 on the attractions map on the inside back cover of this work).

Promised Valley Playhouse, 132 South State Street, (801) 364-5696, (801) 84111 (number 16 on the attractions map on the inside back cover of this work).

City and County Building, between 4th and 5th South State Street, 533-0858 is a classic building that merits a visit (number 35 on the attractions map on the inside back cover of this work). National Registry of Historic Places, 1891-1894.

Utah State Capitol, Capitol Hill, 538-3000 is another building worth a visit (number 21 on the attractions map on the inside back cover of this work).

ENTERTAINMENT

Hogle Zoo, 2600 East Sunnyside Avenue, (801) 582-1631.

The 49th Street Galleria has indoor miniature golf, a bowling center, roller skating rink, batting cages, rides for small children, arcade, and eateries. Take the 53rd South Street off ramp from I-80, drive west to 700 West Street and turn right or north. 700 West Street becomes Murray Blvd. Just after it crosses Vine Street turn right on the first street, which becomes the freeway frontage road in front of the Galleria, 4998 South 360 West Street, Murray 84118, (801) 265-3866.

Lagoon is a well-landscaped summer amusement park with rides, water slides and swimming pools, 375 North Highway 91, Farmington 84025, (801) 451-8000.

Raging Waters (20 water slides, 11 swimming pools, waves, etc.), 1200 West 1700 South Street, 84104, (801) 973-9900.

Classic Skating Center and Waterslides (roller skating, water slides, etc., 9151 South 255 West Street, Sandy, (801) 561-1791.

Classic Roller Skating, 2774 South 625 West Street, Bountiful (801) 295-8301.

The Sports Park (batting cages, mini-golf, video arcade, and race cars), 8695 South Sandy Parkway (west of I-15 on 90th South, (801) 562-4444.

SPECTATOR SPORTS

Utah Jazz (Basketball Team) Ticket Office, Salt Palace (801) 355-3865. Games are played in the Delta Center, 300 West South Temple

Street (number 32 on the attractions map on the inside back cover of this work).

Golden Eagles Hockey Club, 5 Triad Center, (801) 521-6120. Games are played in the Delta Center, 300 West South Temple Street (number 32 on the attractions map on the inside back cover of this work).

Salt Lake Trappers Baseball Club Ticket Office (801) 484-9901. Stadium is located at 1300 South West Temple Street.

GOLF COURSES - PUBLIC (Listed in order of proximity to the Library):

Nibley Park Golf Course, 2780 South 700 East Street, 84106, (801) 483-5418. Nine holes and driving range.

Rose Park Golf Course, 1386 North Redwood Road, 84116, (801) 596-5030. Eighteen holes and driving range.

Glendale Golf Course, 1630 West 2100 South, 84119, (801) 974-2403. Eighteen holes and driving range.

Mountain Dell Golf Course, Parleys Canyon, 84106, (801) 582-3812. Thirty-six holes and driving range.

GYMNASIUMS (Listed in order of proximity to the Library):

Deseret Gymnasium, 161 North Main Street, (801) 359-3911. Basketball, handball, racquetball and squash courts; climbing wall; exercise and weight rooms; and indoor pools.

Sports Mall, Crossroads Plaza, 50 South Main Street, 84144, (801) 328-3116. Indoor and outdoor tennis courts, basketball, handball, and racquetball.

Sightseeing and Entertainment

SKI RESORTS (Listed in order of proximity to the Library). Utah's license plates read, "The Greatest Snow on Earth":

Solitude Ski Resort (Big Cottonwood Canyon SR-190), P.O. Box 21350, Salt Lake City, UT 84121-0350, (801) 534-1000, FAX (801) 649-5276, 23 miles from the Library.

Brighton Ski Resort (Big Cottonwood Canyon SR-190), Star Route, Brighton, UT 84121, (801) 943-8309, FAX (801) 649-1787, 25 miles from the Library.

Snowbird Ski and Summer Resort (Little Cottonwood Canyon SR-210), Snowbird, UT 84092-6019, (801) 742-2222 (800 453-3000), FAX (801) 742-3300, 26 miles from the Library.

Alta Ski Lifts (Little Cottonwood Canyon SR-210), Alta, UT 84092, (801) 742-3333, Snow Report (801) 572-3939, 27 miles from the Library.

Park City Ski Area, P.O. Box 39, Park City, UT 84060, (801) 649-8111, Snow Report (801) 649-9571, FAX (801) 649-5964, 30 miles from the Library.

Deer Valley, P.O. Box 1525, Park City, UT 84060, (801) 649-1000, FAX (801) 649-1910, 38 miles from the Library.

Bus transportation to all resorts is available seven days a week for skiers via Lewis Bros. Stages, (801) 359-8677 (800 826-5844); Ski Bus Express, (801) 975-0202; Ski Bus (801) 262-5626.

MALLS (Listed in order of proximity to the Library):

Crossroads Plaza Shopping Center, 50 South Main Street, (801) 363-1558. The Crossroads Plaza Mall is shown as number 14 on the attractions map on the inside back cover of this work.

ZCMI Center 36 South State Street, (801) 321-8743 (number 13 on the attractions map on the inside back cover of this work). The cornice and

Chapter 15

cast iron facade, 15 South Main Street, dating from the earlier 1901 building, is on the National Registry of Historic Places.

Trolley Square, 602 East 500 South Street, (801) 521-9877.

Valley Fair Mall, 3601 South 2700 West Street, West Valley City, (801) 969-6211.

Cottonwood Mall, 4835 South Highland Drive 84117, (801) 278-0416.

Fashion Place, 6191 South State Street, Murray (801) 265-0504.

South Towne Mall, 10450 South State Street, Sandy (801) 571-5492.

SUMMARY:

A little relaxation is good for clearing the mind, lifting the soul and refreshing the body.

"The accustomed coach life began again, now, and by midnight it almost seemed as if we never had been out of our snuggery among the mail-sacks at all. We had made one alteration, however. We had provided enough bread, boiled ham, and hard-boiled eggs to last double the six hundred miles of staging we had still to do.

"And it was comfort in those succeeding days to sit up and contemplate the majestic panorama of mountains and valleys spread out below us and eat ham and hard-boiled eggs while our spiritual natures reveled alternately in rainbows, thunder-storms, and peerless sunsets."

-- Mark Twain, *Roughing It* (New York: Grosset & Dunlap, 1913), page 85. Originally published: New York: American Publishing Co., 1871. Twain visited Salt Lake City in 1861.

Chapter 16

SIGHTS ALONG THE HIGHWAYS
TO SALT LAKE CITY

INTERSTATE 15 FROM LOS ANGELES AND LAS VEGAS

A colorful, scenic side loop trip of twenty-two extra miles is through the fee-free **Valley of Fire State Park** east off of I-15. Thirty-six miles northeast of Las Vegas turn east to the Park. After driving through the Park you join SR-169 (state route) near Lake Mead south of Overton and rejoin I-15 three miles northeast of the Moapa I-15 exit. An enjoyable side trip in the cool months of the year.

The buffet at the **Peppermill Resort Hotel & Casino,** Mesquite, Nevada, (702) 346-5232, (800 621-0187), is one of the finest and very reasonable; even cheaper nice meals are available from its menu.

Don't miss taking a little closer look at the grandeur of the **Virgin River Narrows** as you leave Littlefield, Arizona traveling I-15 to St. George, Utah.

A very short but memorable side trip is to drive west out of St. George through Santa Clara to **Snow Canyon State Park** and return to St. George from the north on SR-18.

No one should miss seeing **Zion Canyon** in Zion National Park. Years ago, when I worked as a desk clerk at the Lodge, as an eastern tourist registered he exclaimed, "It's beautiful. Zion is Yosemite in color!" Zion is particularly beautiful and interesting in a rain storm, as the moisture changes the canyon walls into darker colors, and dry rivulets above the cliffs come alive and spill colored waterfalls into the canyon. It is a sixty-four mile round trip off the interstate on SR-9, open all year. If you can't spare the time to see the main canyon, at least take the fourteen-mile round trip into **Kolob Canyon,** near New Harmony and Kanarraville. Kolob Canyon is open in the summer months.

Chapter 16

There is no fee to see the spectacular scenery of Kolob Canyon, just off I-15 at exit 40, thirty-two miles northeast of St. George and seventeen miles south of Cedar City. The seven-mile drive rises from 5,054 feet at the visitors center just off I-15 to 6,401 feet at the last, and highest, Kolob Canyon Viewpoint.

The **Shakespearean Festival**, which also includes contemporary plays, is held on the campus of Southern Utah State College at Cedar City and is a worthwhile mid-July through August stop. For their schedule write The Utah Shakespearean Festival, 351 West Center, Cedar City, Utah 84720, (801) 586-7880. An extra treat is to dine at the **Black Swan**, with its Shakespearean era decor, costumed staff, etc., 164 South 100 West Street, Cedar City, UT 84720, (801) 586-7673, lunch summers only, dinner year round, closed Sundays year round and Mondays during the school year.

Colorful **Cedar Breaks National Monument**, with its magnificent vista overlooking Kolob Terrace and Zion National Park, is a scenic twenty-three mile summer loop trip via SR-14 from Cedar City and SR-143 to Parowan. You climb from an elevation of 5,840 at Cedar City to 9,900 in about fifteen miles.

Alpine Scenic Loop, SR-92, off US-189 in Provo Canyon, is a spectacular twenty-nine mile summer loop trip that climbs to an altitude of over 9,000 feet behind 11,750 foot Mt. Timpanogos and descends through American Fork Canyon back to the 4,500 foot elevation of Utah Valley.

Timpanogos Cave National Monument is a adventurous summer excursion for amateur spelunkers, no ropes or flashlights. However, it is a strenuous three-mile round trip hike up the side of American Fork Canyon to the cave. Early weekday morning visits are the coolest and best, as waiting lists are created because tours can only accommodate a limited number of people.

Historical sites along I-15 include the **Brigham Young Winter Home** in St. George; **Old Silver Reef** mining town at Leeds; **Old Cove Fort**; and Utah's **first territorial capitol** in Fillmore.

Southern Californians and Nevadans might sometime extend their research trip to the Family History Library with a lengthy return sightseeing trip to **Dinosaur National Monument** via US-40, Split Rock and Harpers Point in Colorado for a spectacular view of the confluence of the Green and Yampa Rivers. Then on to Rangely, Colorado on SR-64 and to Grand Junction on SR-139. Just out of Grand Junction is **Colorado National Monument** that is a worthwhile short side trip. Westward bound on I-70 turn off at Cisco and follow the Colorado River down its beautiful canyon to Moab. Take side trips from Moab sixteen miles to **Arches National Park** and another sixty miles to **Dead Horse Point State Park**. Continue south from Moab on US-191 with a sixty-eight mile round trip into Squaw Flat of **Canyon Lands National Park**. The road passes through **Newspaper Rock State Historical Monument**. At Blanding then take SR-95 to **Natural Bridges National Monument** and on to Hanksville, with a side trip up to **Goblin Valley State Reserve** on SR-24. West out of Hanksville on SR-24 tour **Capitol Reef National Park**. Turn south on SR-12 at Torrey to Boulder, Escalante, Tropic, and Ruby's Inn. Take an awesome side trip into **Bryce Canyon National Park**. From Bryce drive to Panguitch and turn south and southwest into the Dixie National Forest and on to **Cedar Breaks National Monument**. Since you stopped at **Kolob Canyon** on the way to Salt Lake City, drive east out of **Cedar Breaks** to US-89 south to the Mount Carmel Junction and on into **Zion National Park**, up to the Narrows and a cool, very easy two-mile round trip hike along the Virgin River into the depths of one of the nation's wonders. The last sight to see would be **Snow Canyon State Park**, page 163, if you didn't see it on the way to Salt Lake City. A total of thirteen western wonders in just a few days, a glorious trip. A nice way to unwind from a heavy research trip to the Family History Library.

US-89 FROM PHOENIX AND FLAGSTAFF

Grand Canyon's South and North rims are notable side trips on this route to Salt Lake City. At least one of the rim trips is a must. The South rim can be visited by an eighty-eight mile loop trip via scenic US-180 and SR-64, all year. The North Rim is open in the summer and is an eighty-three mile partial loop trip.

Chapter 16

Zion National Park is a forty-six mile round trip on SR-9 from the Mount Carmel Junction and, as explained above, is well worth the trip. The Mount Carmel entrance to the Park is considered by many visitors to be more spectacular than the valley entrance via St. George.

Bryce Canyon National Park is a thirty-four mile round trip off the route and is an unforgettable experience. It is open all year.

The Big Rock Candy Mountain merits learning the folk song about it (before you leave home) and a stop to look, see, and sing.

STATE ROUTE 44 AND US HIGHWAYS 64, 550, 160, 666, 191, AND 6, FROM ALBUQUERQUE

Southwest Colorado offers many wonderful scenic places to visit on two different routes to Salt Lake City. The **San Juan Mountains** provide a beautiful summer drive up US-550 to US-50 and on to I-70 at Grand Junction, Colorado. The second starts on SR-44 at Bloomfield, New Mexico. Then on to Aztec, Durango, Silverton, and over 11,018 foot Red Mountain Pass to Ouray, Montrose, and Grand Junction.

Mesa Verde National Park is a sixty-two mile round trip east off of US-666 east of Cortez, Colorado and a unique summer day trip.

Arches National Park's visitors center is right next to US-666, eight miles north of Moab. This beautiful park is open all year. A lot of the park may be seen from park roads, but a little hiking is required to see its better natural arches.

INTERSTATE 70 FROM DENVER

Colorado National Monument is only a few extra miles loop trip from Grand Junction to Fruita, Colorado, and well worth the time.

Arches National Park is a fifty-four mile round trip south of the interstate. It is an interesting park, open all year.

164

Goblin Valley State Reserve is further off the interstate. It is less well known, but very interesting for a summer visit because of its unique formations. A few miles of the route into the park is dirt. For desert lovers the dirt road drive from there northwest rejoining the interstate via the **San Rafael Swell** is a very exciting and colorful dry weather trip. However, you should return to Green River, as the shortest route to Salt Lake City is via US-6 and US-191.

US-40 FROM DENVER

Dinosaur National Monument, near Vernal, offers two spectacular sights. One in Colorado requires a moderate two-mile hike to Harpers Corner Overlook to view the confluence of the Yampa and Green Rivers. The other is Split Mountain on the Green River in Utah at the Split Mountain campground. Of course, the open-all-year Dinosaur Quarry Visitor Center is a must for everyone.

INTERSTATE 80 FROM ROCK SPRINGS AND CHEYENNE

History abounds on this route. It was the **Mormon Trail** and the route of the Donner Party from **Fort Bridger** west. The scenery down the canyons to the Salt Lake Valley is also super.

Sometime while driving from the east on I-80 all researchers should take time to leave I-80 at Ogallala, Nebraska and travel along the North Platte River, the **Oregon and Mormon Trails** via US-26 past **Courthouse and Jail Rocks, Chimney Rock, Scottsbluff,** and **Fort Laramie.** Continue on near the trail route on I-25 to Casper, then on SR-220 past **Independence Rock** and **Devils Gate** and on US-287 to SR-20 through **South Pass.** Please stop and read the **Whitman monument.** At Farson turn south to Rock Springs and rejoin I-80. You meet the **California and Mormon Trails** at Fort Bridger.

The following narrative histories and trail guides are recommended for background reading for the above tour:

165

Chapter 16

Parkman, Francis. *The Oregon Trail.* New York: Penguin Books, 1982. Paper $4.95. Penguin Books, P.O. Box 120, Bergenfield, NJ 07621-0120, (201) 387-0600 (800 526-0275).
Originally published as *The California and Oregon Trail.* New York: Putnam, 1849.

Stewart, George Rippey. *The California Trail: An Epic with Many Heroes.* Lincoln: University of Nebraska Press, 1983. Paper $9.95. University of Nebraska Press, 901 North 17th Street, Room 327, Lincoln, NE 68588-0520, (800) 755-1105.
Originally published: New York: McGraw-Hill, 1962.

Hafen, Le Roy Reuben, and Hafen, Ann W. *Handcarts to Zion: The Story of a Unique Western Migration, 1856-1860: With Contemporary Journals, Accounts, Reports, and Rosters of Members of the Ten Handcart Companies.* Lincoln: University of Nebraska Press in Association with the A. H. Clarke Co., 1992. Paper $9.95. University of Nebraska Press, 901 North 17th Street, Room 327, Lincoln, NE 68588-0520, (800) 755-1105.
Originally published: Glendale, Calif.: A. H. Clarke Co., 1960.

Franzwa, Gregory M. *The Oregon Trail Revisited.* 4th ed. St. Louis, Mo.: Patrice Press, 1988. $14.95, paper $7.95. Patrice Press, 1701 South Eight Street, Saint Louis, MO 63104, (800) 367-9242.

INTERSTATE 80 FROM WENDOVER AND RENO

Lots of people dislike this route to Salt Lake City. However, others find the mountains of Nevada and the salt flats of Utah interesting and even picturesque.

As the **Ruby Mountains** east of Elko come into view you are looking at some of the most beautiful mountains in Nevada. Nestled high on their eastern slope is a quiet little lake, **Angel Lake**. A good two lane paved road can take you on a scenic twenty-four mile round trip to Angel Lake out of Wells.

If Nevada's mountains and desert have gotten to you by the time you reach Wendover, a delicious oasis is the buffet at the **Peppermill Inn & Casino**, Wendover, Nevada, (702) 664-2255. It is one of the finest and very reasonable; even cheaper nice meals are available from its menu.

East of Wendover the **Bonneville Speedway** is a disappointment most of the year because it is under water. Nevertheless, to the person who would like to say that he or she has been there, it is worth the twelve-mile round trip. National Registry of Historic Places, 1911.

The **Bonnevile Salt Flats Rest Area** just east of Wendover is the safest place to park and check out the salt. Yes, it really is salt, but not fit for consumption on hard boiled eggs at your picnic.

Twenty-six miles east of the state line is a salt flat sculpture with two titles, **"Desert Tree Art Sculpture" and/or "Tree of Utah,"** the creation of Karl Momen, a Swedish sculptor and architect. It was erected in 1984, eight-three feet tall, concrete, and weighing two hundred tons.* Disliked by some, liked by others, and laughed at by many, it is usually a welcome relief from the bright sun and mirages that make it appear as if you'll drive straight into the lake at any moment. Most people ask, "What is that sculpture doing way out here?" Others just say, "Far out!"

    -- * May, Fred E., and Wilkerson, Bill. *Interstate 80: The Historic Route, Salt Lake City, Utah, to Reno, Nevada.* Layton, Utah: Travel Geografix, 1991, page 12.

Sometime on a homeward bound trip the adventurous Californian or Nevadan may wish to take in the **Pony Express route** south of I-80. The scenic route is to take I-15 to Lehi, SR-73 with a brief stop at **Cedar Fort** and the **Stagecoach Inn** to read the historical markers and see the sites, National Registry of Historic Places, 1858. Then on to SR-36 and SR-199 over Johnson Pass to Dugway. At the Dugway Proving Grounds entrance you turn left and explore some of the finest Pony Express station ruins in the West. There is an oasis at **Fish Springs National Wildlife Reserve.** Take all the food and water you may need for nearly an all day trip, as well as a tank full of gas. Don't miss Callao. You may also wish to detour to Gold Hill and Ibapah. By the way, the road is good graded gravel, fine for a sedan in fair weather and well worth the trip. Once, that is. If you love the desert it's an interesting trip; if you don't love the desert, don't go. And, by the way, it's over a hundred miles. Rejoin I-80 at Wendover or go on to Ely via White Horse Pass on US-Alt 93 to US 93 and US-50 for a more scenic route west, cheaper motel rates, more **Pony Express station ruins** and sites, and some unique bars that serve great grilled cheese sandwiches for tired bicyclists. My pedaling son suggests that I explain this last remark as he, at fourteen, with his older brother and me, took ten days to pedal to Provo, Utah from Turlock, California via California SR-4, SR-88, and US-50. They went to a high school debate workshop at Brigham Young University and I to teach at a genealogy workshop, followed by research at the Family History Library. It was a fun, real adventure. The widely spaced bars were to cyclists as stage stations to earlier travelers, but improved considerably, with cold soft drinks, grills, and shade in which to rest.

If you are not intrigued to drive around the southern edge of the Great Salt Lake, at least have someone in the auto read aloud the following book as you travel homeward on I-80:

> Stewart, George Rippey. *The California Trail: An Epic with Many Heroes*. Lincoln: University of Nebraska Press, 1983. Paper $9.95. University of Nebraska Press, 901 North 17th Street, Room 327, Lincoln, NE 68588-0520, (800) 755-1105.
> Originally published: New York: McGraw-Hill, 1962.

US-50 FROM ELY AND CARSON CITY, NEVADA

Lehman Caves, which is part of the **Great Basin National Park**, near the Utah border, is well worth the nine-mile partial loop drive. The cave is open all year and has a great number of marvelous formations; an easy walk but lots of stairs.

Wheeler Peak is another (summer only) twenty-mile round trip above Lehman Caves, where a moderate five-mile round trip hike takes you to one of the few **bristle cone pine** forests in the world. If you do not wish to hike, the drive provides a marvelous view of Utah's western desert from the white pine forest near the 10,000 foot level of the 13,063 foot peak.

Night driving on this route is somewhat hazardous, because it passes through open cattle range and the warm roadways attract livestock at night.

INTERSTATES 84, 15, AND US-89 FROM IDAHO

The **Great Salt Lake** is visible from several points south of Ogden along these routes. A sunset view of the Great Salt Lake from the mountain slopes east of any of the communities from Roy to Bountiful is one of the most marvelous sunset sights in the world.

ROADSIDE GUIDES

Guides to the sights along a highway and the local history of the area traveled are interesting to many travelers. The following are some that can turn travel into an informative experience:

Roylance, Ward Jay. *Utah: A Guide to the State, Part 2, Tour Section.* Revised and enlarged. Salt Lake City: *Utah: A Guide to the State* Foundation, 1982 ($9.95 paper, 506 pages; available from the Western Epics Publishing Co., 254 South Main Street, Salt Lake City, UT 84101, (801) 328-2586).

May, Fred E., and Wilkerson, Bill. *Interstate 80: Reno, Nevada, to Salt Lake City, Utah. Eastbound Version, 523 Miles of Fascinating Information, History - Geography - Legends - Animal Life - Geology.* Layton, Utah: Travel Geografix, 1992 ($9.95 paper, 78 pages; available from the Travel Geografix, 439 North Spring Valley Parkway East, Elko NV 89801, (702) 753-8335).

May, Fred E., and Wilkerson, Bill. *Interstate 80: The Historic Route, Salt Lake City, Utah, to Reno, Nevada. Westbound Version for Enroute Travelers.* Layton, Utah: Travel Geografix, 1991 ($9.95 paper, 74 pages).

169

Chapter 16

May, Fred E., and Wilkerson, Bill. *Milepost Guidebook to Interstate 15: Las Vegas, Nevada, to Salt Lake City, Utah. Northbound Version.* Layton, Utah: Travel Geografix, in progress ($9.95 paper).

May, Fred E., and Wilkerson, Bill. *Milepost Guidebook to Interstate 15: Salt Lake City, Utah to Las Vegas, Nevada. Southbound Version.* Layton, Utah: Travel Geografix, in progress ($9.95 paper).

Trimble, Marshall. *Roadside History of Arizona.* Missoula, Mont.: Mountain Press Pub. Co., 1986 ($12.95, 480 pages, P.O. Box 2399, 59806, (406) 728-1900, (800) 234-5308).

McTighe, James *Roadside History of Colorado.* Rev. ed. Boulder, Colo.: Johnson Books, 1989 ($11.95 paper, 628 pages, 1880 South 57th Court, 80301, (303) 443-1576, (800) 662-2665).

Wilson, D. Ray. *Kansas Historical Tour Guide.* 2d ed. Carpentersville, Ill.: Crossroads Communications, 1990 ($9.95 paper, 346 pages, P.O. Box 7, 60110-0007, (708) 426-0008).

West, Carroll Van. *A Traveler's Companion to Montana History.* Helena, Mont.: Montana Historical Society Press, 1986 ($9.95 paper, 239 pages, 225 North Roberts Street, Helena, MT 59620, (406) 444-2890).

Boye, Alan. *The Complete Roadside Guide to Nebraska.* St. Johnsbury, Vt.: Saltillo Press, 1989 ($11.95 paper, 370 pages, 57 Lafayette, 05819).

Fugate, Francis L. and Fugate, Roberta B. *Roadside History of New Mexico.* Missoula, Mont.: Mountain Press Pub. Co., 1989 ($24.95, $15.95 paper, 483 pages).

Wilson, D. Ray. *Wyoming Historical Tour Guide.* 2d ed. Carpentersville, Ill.: Crossroads Communications, 1990 ($9.95, 264 pages).

THE GEOLOGICAL SCENE

Because the geological formations of the West are so exposed to view, amateur geologists and geographers can have an exciting field trip driving to Salt Lake City if they utilize one of the many available field guides that are included in the following list:

Chronic, Halka. *Roadside Geology of Utah.* Missoula Mont.: Mountain Press, 1990 ($12.95 paper, 326 pages, P.O. Box 2399, 59806, (406) 728-1900, (800) 234-5308).

Chronic, Halka. *Roadside Geology of Arizona.* Missoula Mont.: Mountain Press, 1983 ($12.95 paper, 321 pages).

Hamblin, W. Kenneth. *Roadside Geology of U.S. Interstate 80 Between Salt Lake City and San Francisco: The Meaning Behind the Landscape.* Sponsored by the American Geological Institute. Van Nuys, Calif.: Varna Enterprises, 1974 ($5.00 paper, 51 pages, American Geological Institute, 4220 King Street, Alexandria VA 22302-1507, (703) 379-2480, (800) 336-4764).

Alt, David D., and Hyndman, Donald W. *Roadside Geology of Northern California.* Missoula, Mont.: Mountain Press Pub. Co., 1975 ($11.95 paper, 244 pages).

Sharp, Robert Phillip. *Field Guide, Southern California.* 2d Rev. ed. K/H Geology Field Guide Series. Dubuque, Iowa: Kendall/Hunt, 1990 ($15.95 paper, 208 pages, 2460 Kerper Blvd, 52001, (319) 588-1451, (800) 338-578).

Chronic, Halka. *Roadside Geology of Colorado.* Missoula Mont.: Mountain Press, 1980 ($11.95 paper, 334 pages).

Alt, David D., and Hyndman, Donald W. *Roadside Geology of Idaho.* Roadside Geology Series. Missoula: Mountain Press Pub. Co., 1989 ($14.95, 393 pages).

Chapter 16

Alt, David D., and Hyndman, Donald W. *Roadside Geology of Montana*. Missoula: Mountain Press Pub. Co., 1986 ($12.95 paper, 427 pages).

Chronic, Halka. *Roadside Geology of New Mexico*. Missoula Mont.: Mountain Press, 1986 ($9.95 paper).

Alt, David D., and Hyndman, Donald W. *Roadside Geology of Oregon*. Roadside Geology Series. Missoula, Mont.: Mountain Press Pub. Co., 1978 ($11.95 paper, 279 pages).

Alt, David D., and Hyndman, Donald W. *Roadside Geology of Washington*. Missoula, Mont. Mountain Press Pub. Co., 1984 ($12.95 paper, 282 pages).

Lageson, David R., and Spearing, Darwin. *Roadside Geology of Wyoming*. Missoula, Mont. Mountain Press Pub. Co., 1988 ($9.95 paper, 274 pages).

This section of *Going* is dedicated to Walter ("Uncle Walt") R. Buss, who thirty-nine years ago introduced the author to field and roadside guides while he was a geology and geography student of "Uncle Walt's" at Weber College (now Weber State University). Now retired, "Uncle Walt" is still an avid geologist and geographer, but now is also an avid genealogist.

ADDITIONAL READING:

American Automobile Association. *Colorado/Utah*. Heathrow, Fla.: American Automobile Association, 1991.

SUMMARY:

Take some time to relax and drink in the beauties of the still somewhat-wild West as you drive to and from Salt Lake City and the Family History Library.

PART III

BACK HOME AGAIN

Chapter 17

REVIEW, FOLLOW-UP, AND GOING ON

After a visit to the Family History Library make sure that you review your research and add to your pedigrees and family group sheets the information obtained in Salt Lake City. There's a saying that for every hour you spend in the Library you need to devote two hours to studying your findings. Take time to analyze the fruits of your labors, prepare for additional research, and plan for future trips to Salt Lake City and other cities where you may need to continue your research.

Write to people you found who may also be researching your lines. Write county courthouses for records not available in the Family History Library. It may be necessary to hire someone in a county seat if the county court house staff is not helpful.

It may also be necessary to write for certificates of birth, marriage, or death for ancestors who were born, married, or who died in the twentieth century. The addresses and fees of the various United States vital records offices are listed in the U.S. National Center for Health Statistics, *Where to Write for Vital Records: Births, Deaths, Marriages, and Divorces* (Hyattsville, Md.: 1990). Many Family History Centers and public libraries also have Thomas Jay Kemp's *International Vital Records Handbook* (Baltimore: Genealogical Publishing Co., 1990) that provides the forms often needed for obtaining certificates of vital records. His book also includes addresses, fees, and telephone numbers for vital records offices in the United States, Canada, the United Kingdom, and Ireland. For addresses of other foreign offices, various how-to-do-it genealogical research books and other resources at your local Family History Center can be of assistance. Before submitting requests to a vital records office in the United States, it is wise to telephone the office. Many of them have recorded messages providing current prices and the latest restrictions concerning the availability of records.

Chapter 17

Share your research through gifts of family histories, pedigrees and family group sheets to relatives and others who may ask for your assistance. Submit your family group sheets and pedigrees to the *Ancestral File* and send in corrections if you find errors in it (refer again to chapter 4 for details).

If your first visit to the Family History Library was not as productive as you might have wished, you may need better preparation. Perhaps more use of a Family History Center could fill those needs. Reading additional how-to-do-it books may help. Seminars, workshops, or programs offered by local genealogical societies have helped numerous researchers. Return to the Family History Library with a group that has experienced researchers who are willing to share their expertise with you.

If you are over sixty years of age you are eligible, along with your companion of at least age fifty, to enroll in any of the Elderhostel beginning genealogy programs in Provo, Utah, offered by the Brigham Young University, and their advanced courses in Salt Lake City at the Family History Library. In Provo you will have the opportunity for both instruction and daily research in the large campus Family History Center, and, in some courses, assistance in a field trip to the Family History Library. Recent courses in Provo included:

> Beginning Genealogy Library Research
> Beginning Genealogy Workshop
> Beginning Genealogy Workshop for the Deaf
> British Isles Research Workshop
> Composing Your Personal History
> Computer Genealogy
> Genealogy Library Research
> Germany: The Many and the One
> Intermediate Genealogy Library Research
> Intermediate Genealogy Workshop
> Personal Ancestral File: Genealogical Management System
>   for Home Computers
> Preservation of Genealogical Records with Computers
> Reading Early American Handwriting

Write Elderhostel, 75 Federal Street, Boston, MA 02110, (617) 426-8056, for their catalog. Programs currently offered may not continue because of low enrollment, instructors' interest changes, and site administration turnover.

Elderhostel courses in genealogy are also offered at numerous other colleges, universities, and educational centers in Canada and the United States. Those listed in recent Elderhostel catalogs were:

> University of South Alabama, Baldwin County, Beachside, Alabama
> Stillman College, Tuscaloosa, Alabama
> Rio Salado Community College, Phoenix East Valley, Tempe, Arizona
> Pikes Peak Community College, Colorado Springs, Colo.
> University of Delaware, Lewes, Delaware
> Deerhaven Camp and Conference Center, Deerhaven, Fla.
> Central Florida Community College, Ocala, Florida
> Centerbury Retreat and Conference Center, Oviedo, Fla.
> Simpsonwood Conference Center, Atlanta, Georgia
> Calvin Center, near Atlanta, Georgia
> Columbus College, Columbus, Georgia
> Georgia College, Milledgeville, Georgia
> Waldorf College, Forest City, Kansas
> University of Kentucky, Louisville, Kentucky
> Boston College/New England Historic Genealogical Society, Chestnut Hill, Massachusetts
> Heartland Presbyterian Center, Weston, Missouri
> Cape May Institute, Wildwood, New Jersey
> Stella Niagara Education Park, Center of Renewal, Niagara Falls, New York
> Holiday Hills Conference Center, YMCA, Pawling, N.Y.
> Roberts Wesleyan College, Rochester, New York
> Ohio University, Athens, Ohio
> Valley Forge Historical Society, Valley Forge National Historical Park, Pennsylvania
> Winthrop University, Rock Hill, South Carolina
> University of Texas, Austin, Texas
> Lamar University, Beaumont, Texas

Northern Virginia 4-H Educational Center, Front Royal,
    Virginia
Mary Baldwin College, Staunton, Virginia
Centralia College/St. Mary's Center, Toledo, Wash.
George Williams College, Lake Geneva, Wisconsin
Grande Prairie Regional College, Alberta, Canada
Alberni Valley Community Program, Port Alberni, British
    Columbia, Canada
Dalhousie University, Nova Scotia, Canada
Canterbury Hills Conference Centre, Hamilton, Ontario,
    Canada
O'Connor House, Ottawa, Ontario, Canada
Luther Village, Kenora, Ontario, Canada
Ottawa YM-YWCA, Ottawa, Ontario, Canada
The Bruce Connection, Port Elgin, Ontario, Canada

I. FAMILY HISTORY CENTER USERS:

Order microforms that you did not have time to read while in Salt Lake
City.

II. LOCAL PUBLIC LIBRARY USERS:

Request your reference librarian to interlibrary loan some of the printed
materials or census schedules you were not able to read while in Salt
Lake City. One example would be to request photocopies of
biographical sketches through the interlibrary loan services of your
public library. Provide the librarian with the author, title, place of
publication, publisher, date of publication, beginning page, and name of
biographee. If any library's interlibrary loan service prohibits obtaining
a photocopy of a desired biographical sketch, ask for a copy of the
American Library Directory. Locate the name and address of the state,
county, city or regional library serving the geographical locale of
interest. Write to the library directly asking if they will photocopy the
biographical sketch for you.

Many libraries are able to obtain microfilm copies of the U.S. federal census schedules through interlibrary loan from their state libraries or through the rental services of the National Archives Microfilm Rental Program, P.O. Box 30, Annapolis Junction, MD 20701-0030, (301) 604-3699 or the American Genealogical Lending Library, P.O. Box 244, Bountiful, Utah 84011, (801) 298-5358 (800 657-9442), FAX (801) 298-5468.

The U.S. National Center for Health Statistics, *Where to Write for Vital Records: Births, Deaths, Marriages, and Divorces* (Hyattsville, Md.: 1990) mentioned above is usually available in your local public library and in some public libraries may be available under the government publications classification number, HE20.6210/2:990. If your public library does not have it, the U.S. Depository Library in your nearest university library or larger public library probably has it.

III. HOME LIBRARY USERS:

It may be necessary to join some of the book or microfilm home loan programs that are advertised in various genealogical journals. The largest and most reasonable rental collection is owned by the American Genealogical Lending Library, P.O. Box 244, Bountiful UT 84011, (801) 298-5358 (800 657-9442), FAX (801) 298-5468. They have over 100,000 microforms in their rental collection, including all of the U.S. federal census schedules; state census schedules; nearly all of the U.S. ship passenger lists; and many military records, family histories, and county histories.

The U.S. National Center for Health Statistics, *Where to Write for Vital Records: Births, Deaths, Marriages, and Divorces* (Hyattsville, Md.: 1990) mentioned above may be obtained for your home use for $1.75 from the Superintendent of Documents, U.S. Government Printing Office, Washington, D.C. 20402 (stock number 017-022-01109-3).

Chapter 17

ADDITIONAL READING:

All of the following are available at the Family History Library and its Centers.

FamilySearch: Contributing Information to Ancestral File". Salt Lake City: Corporation of the President of The Church Jesus Christ of Latter-day Saints, 1990. 4 pages.

FamilySearch: Correcting Information in Ancestral File". Series AF, No. 4. Salt Lake City: Corporation of the President of The Church Jesus Christ of Latter-day Saints, 1991. 4 pages.

SUMMARY:

After a visit to the Family History Library, it is necessary to review, update, analyze, plan for additional research trips, write to others researching your lines, and request additional materials through the interlibrary loan services of a Family History Center, a public library, or through home loan programs. Also share your completed research with others by contributing to the *FamilySearch: Ancestral File.*

> "Look at all of these marvelous records that my cousin sent me!"
> -- Turlock, California researcher, 1992

APPENDIX

FAMILY HISTORY CENTERS
IN THE UNITED STATES AND CANADA

Below is a list of cities, arranged by state or province, in which a Family History Center is located. Some of them are listed in your telephone book under the Church of Jesus Christ of Latter-day Saints (either white, yellow, or business pages); if not listed call Tuesday through Saturday evenings or Sundays any of the numbers listed under the Church of Jesus Christ of Latter-day Saints. If you are not able to contact anyone at the Church, call your local public library, local genealogical society, or write or call the Family History Library, 35 North West Temple Street, Salt Lake City UT 84150 (801) 240-2331 to locate the Center serving your area. Cities listed with a number following have more than one Center. There are currently 668 Family History Centers in Canada and the United States.

ALABAMA

Bessemer
Birmingham
Dothan
Huntsville
Mobile
Montgomery

ALASKA

Anchorage
Fairbanks
Juneau
Ketchikan
Kotzebue
Sitka
Soldotna
Wasilla

ARIZONA

Buckeye
Casa Grande
Cottonwood
Eagar
Flagstaff
Globe
Holbrook
Kingman
Mesa
Nogales
Page
Peoria
Phoenix 7
Prescott
Safford
Scottsdale
Show Low
Sierra Vista

Snowflake
St. David
St. Johns
Tucson
Winslow
Yuma

ARKANSAS

Fort Smith
Jacksonville
Little Rock

CALIFORNIA

Alpine
Anaheim
Anderson
Antioch
Auburn

Appendix

Bakersfield 2
Barstow
Blythe
Buena Park
Camarillo
Canoga Park
Canyon Country
Carlsbad
Cerritos
Chico
Clovis
Concord
Corona
Covina
El Centro
Escondido
Eureka
Fairfield
Fontana
Fresno 3
Glendale
Granada Hills
Gridley
Hacienda Heights
Hanford
Hemet
Huntington Beach
Huntington Park
La Crescenta
Lancaster
Los Alamitos
Los Altos
Los Angeles
Menlo Park
Merced
Mission Viejo
Modesto 2
Monterey Park
Moorpark

Moreno Valley
Mt. Shasta
Napa
Needles
Newbury Park
Norwalk
Oakland
Orange
Palm Desert
Palmdale
Pasadena
Placerville
Quincy
Rancho Palos
Verdes
Redding
Redlands
Reseda
Ridgecrest
Riverside 3
Sacramento
San Bernardino
San Bruno
San Diego 2
San Jose
San Luis Obispo
Santa Barbara
Santa Clara
Santa Cruz
Santa Maria
Santa Rosa
Seaside
Simi Valley
Stockton
Susanville
Torrance
Turlock
Ukiah
Upland

Valencia
Van Nuys
Ventura
Victorville
Visalia
Vista
Westminster
Whittier
Woodland
Yuba City

COLORADO

Alamosa
Arvada
Colorado Springs
Cortez
Craig
Denver
Durango
Fort Collins
Grand Junction
Greeley
La Jara
Littleton 2
Louisville
Montrose
Northglenn
Pueblo

CONNECTICUT

Bloomfield
Madison
New Canaan
Trumbull
Waterford

DELAWARE

Wilmington

FLORIDA

Boca Raton
Ft. Lauderdale
Ft. Myers
Gainsville
Homestead
Jacksonville
Lake City
Lake Mary
Orange Park
Orlando
Panama City
Pensacola
Plantation
Rockledge
St. Petersburg
Tallahassee
Tampa
Winter Haven

GEORGIA

Brunswick
Columbus
Douglas
Gainesville
Jonesboro
Macon
Marietta
Powder Springs
Roswell
Savannah
Tucker

HAWAII

Hilo
Honolulu 2
Kaneohe
Kona
Laie
Lihue
Miliani

IDAHO

Blackfoot 2
Boise 4
Burley
Caldwell
Coeur D'Alene
Driggs
Emmett
Firth
Hailey
Idaho Falls 3
Iona
Lewiston
Malad
Montpelier
Moore
Mountain Home
Nampa
Pocatello
Rexburg
Rigby
Salmon
Sandpoint
Shelley
Soda Springs
Twin Falls
Weiser

ILLINOIS

Champaign
Chicago Heights
Fairview Heights
Naperville
Nauvoo
Peoria
Rockford
Schaumburg
Wilmette

INDIANA

Bloomington
Evansville
Ft. Wayne
Indianapolis
New Albany
Noblesville
South Bend
Terre Haute
West Lafayette

IOWA

Ames
Cedar Rapids
Davenport
Sioux City
West Des Moines

KANSAS

Dodge City
Olathe
Salina
Topeka
Wichita

Appendix

KENTUCKY

Hopkinsville
Lexington
Louisville
Martin
Paducah

LOUISIANA

Alexandria
Baton Rouge
Denham Springs
Monroe
Metairie
Shreveport
Slidell

MAINE

Bangor
Cape Elizabeth
Caribou
Farmingdale

MARYLAND

Annapolis
Ellicott City
Frederick
Kensington
Lutherville

MASSACHUSETTS

Foxboro
Weston
Worcester

MICHIGAN

Ann Arbor
Bloomfield Hills
East Lansing
Grand Blanc
Grand Rapids
Hastings
Kalamazoo
Ludington
Marquette
Midland
Muskegon
Traverse City
Westland

MINNESOTA

Anoka
Duluth
Minneapolis
Rochester
St. Paul

MISSISSIPPI

Clinton
Gulfport
Hattiesburg

MISSOURI

Cape Girardeau
Columbia
Frontenac
Hazelwood
Independence
Joplin
Kansas City

Liberty
Springfield
St. Joseph

MONTANA

Billings 2
Bozeman
Butte
Glasgow
Glendive
Great Falls
Havre
Helena
Kalispell
Missoula
Stevensville

NEBRASKA

Grand Island
Lincoln
Omaha
Papillion

NEVADA

Ely
Elko
Lahonton Valley
Las Vegas
Logandale
Reno
Winnemucca

NEW HAMPSHIRE

Concord
Nashua

NEW JERSEY

Cherry Hill
East Brunswick
Morristown
North Caldwell

NEW MEXICO

Albuquerque 3
Carlsbad
Farmington
Gallup
Grants
Las Cruces
Santa Fe
Silver City

NEW YORK

Binghamton
Jamestown
Lake Placid
Liverpool
Loudonville
New York City
Pittsford
Plainview
Williamsville

NORTH CAROLINA

Charlotte 2
Durham
Fayetteville
Goldsboro
Greensboro
Hickory
Kingston

Raleigh
Skyland
Wilmington
Winston-Salem

NORTH DAKOTA

Bismark
Fargo
Minot

OHIO

Akron
Cincinnati 2
Dayton
Dublin
Fairborn
Kirtland
Reynoldsburg
Toledo
Westlake

OKLAHOMA

Lawton
Muskogee
Norman
Oklahoma City 2
Stillwater
Tulsa

OREGON

Beaverton
Bend
Brookings
Central Point
Coos Bay

Corvallis
Eugene
Grants Pass
Gresham
Hermiston
Hillsboro
Keizer
Klamath Falls
Lagrande
Lake Oswego
Lebanon
McMinnville
Medford
Newport
Nyssa
Ontario
Oregon City
Portland 2
Prineville
Roseburg
Salem 2
Sandy
The Dalles

PENNSYLVANIA

Broomall
Clarks Summit
Erie
Kane
Pittsburgh
Reading
State College
York

**RHODE
ISLAND**

Warwick

Appendix

SOUTH CAROLINA

Charleston
Columbia
Florence
Greenville
North Augusta

SOUTH DAKOTA

Gettysburg
Rapid City
Rosebud
Sioux Falls

TENNESSEE

Chattanooga
Franklin
Kingsport
Knoxville
Madison
Memphis

TEXAS

Abilene
Amarillo
Austin
Bryan
Corpus Christi
Dallas
Denton
Duncanville
El Paso
Fort Worth
Friendswood
Harlingen
Houston 3

Kileen
Kingwood
Longview
Lubbock
McAllen
Odessa
Orange
Pasadena
Plano
Port Arthur
Richland Hills
San Antonio
Sugarland

UTAH

American Fork
Altamont
Beaver
Blanding
Bountiful
Brigham City
Castle Dale
Cedar City
Delta
Duchesne
Ferron
Fillmore
Granger
Heber
Helper
Hunter
Hurricane
Kanab
Kaysville 2
Layton
Lehi
Loa
Logan

Magna 2
Manti
Mapleton
Moab
Monticello
Moroni
Mt. Pleasant
Murray 3
Nephi
Ogden
Panguitch
Parowan
Price
Provo
Provo (BYU)
Richfield
Riverton
Roosevelt
Rose Park
Salt Lake City 5
Sandy 6
Santaquin
South Jordan
Springville
St. George
Tooele
Tremonton
Tropic
Vernal
Wellington
Wendover
West Jordan 2
West Valley City

VERMONT

Berlin

VIRGINIA

Annandale
Bassett
Charlottesville
Chesapeake
Dale City
Falls Church
Fredericksburg
Hamilton
Newport News
Oakton
Pembroke
Richmond
Salem
Virginia Beach
Winchester

WASHINGTON

Auburn
Bellevue
Bremerton
Centralia
Edmonds
Ellensburg
Elma
Ephrata

Everett
Federal Way
Ferndale
Lake Stevens
Longview
Moses Lake
Mount Vernon
North Bend
Olympia
Othello
Pullman
Puyallup
Quincy
Richland
Seattle 2
Silverdale
Spokane 3
Sumner
Tacoma
Vancouver 2
Walla Walla
Wenatchee
Yakima

WEST VIRGINIA

Fairmont
Huntington

WISCONSIN

Eau Claire
Hales Corners
Madison
Shawano

WYOMING

Afton
Casper
Cheyenne
Cody
Evanston
Gillette
Green River
Jackson Hole
Kemmerer
Laramie
Lovell
Rawlins
Riverton
Rock Springs
Sheridan
Urie
Worland

CANADA

ALBERTA

Calgary
Cardston
Edmonton
Grande Prairie
Lethbridge

Raymond
Red Deer
Spruce Grove
Taber

BRITISH COLUMBIA

Burnaby
Courtenay
Cranbrook
Fort St. John

187

Appendix

Kamloops
Kelowna
Prince George
Terrace
Victoria

MANITOBA

Winnipeg

NEW BRUNSWICK

St. John

NOVA SCOTIA

Dartmouth

ONTARIO

Brampton
Chatham
Etobicoke
Fort Frances
Glenburnie
Hamilton
Kitchener
London
Oshawa
Ottawa

Sarnia
Sault St. Marie
St. Thomas
Thunder Bay
Timmins
Windsor

QUEBEC

Montreal 2

SASKATCHEWAN

Regina
Saskatoon

"All of this is free?"

-- An astonished researcher in the
Turlock Family History Center, 1991

SUBJECT INDEX

SALT LAKE CITY DOWNTOWN ACCOMMODATIONS

In Alphabetical Order

	(Area code 801)	Page
Anton Boxrud Bed & Breakfast	363-8035	7
The Avenue's Residential Center	363-8137	3
Best Western Olympus Hotel	521-7373 (800 426-0722)	23
Deseret Inn	532-2900	15
Doubletree Hotel	531-7500 (800 528-0444)	5
Embassy Suites Hotel	359-7800 (800 362-2779)	21
Emerald Inn	533-9300	16
Hilton Hotel	532-3344 (800 445-8667)	14
Holiday Inn - Downtown	532-7000 (800 465-4329)	19
Howard Johnson	521-0130 (800 366-3684 or 800 654-2000	4
The Inn at Temple Square	531-1000	6
The Kimball	363-4000	2
Little America Hotel and Towers	363-6781 (800 453-9450	18
Marriott Hotel	531-0800 (800 228-9290)	8
Mountain City Suites	521-3790 (800 765-8819)	12
Peery Hotel	521-4300	11
Quality Inn - City Center	521-2930 (800 221-2222 or 800 424-6423)	20
Red Lion Hotel	328-2000 (800 547-8010)	10
Residence Inn by Marriott	532-5511 (800 228-9290)	13
Salt Lake City Center TraveLodge	531-7100 (800 255-3050)	17
Salt Lake TraveLodge at Temple Square	533-8200 (800 255-3050)	1
Shilo Inn	521-9500 (800 222-2244)	9
Super 8 Motel	534-0808 (800 843-1991)	22

(Key to downtown accommodations map on page 197)

195

SALT LAKE CITY DOWNTOWN ACCOMMODATIONS

(Key to downtown accommodations map on page 197)

(Area code 801)

1	Salt Lake TraveLodge at Temple Square	
		533-8200 (800 255-3050)
2	The Kimball	363-4000
3	The Avenue's Residential Center	363-8137
4	Howard Johnson 521-0130 (800 366-3684 or 800 654-2000)	
5	Doubletree Hotel	531-7500 (800 528-0444)
6	The Inn at Temple Square	531-1000
7	Anton Boxrud Bed & Breakfast	363-8035
8	Marriott Hotel	531-0800 (800 228-9290)
9	Shilo Inn	521-9500 (800 222-2244)
10	Red Lion Hotel	328-2000 (800 547-8010)
11	Peery Hotel	521-4300
12	Mountain City Suites	521-3790 (800 765-8819)
13	Residence Inn by Marriott	532-5511 (800 228-9290)
14	Hilton Hotel	532-3344 (800 445-8667)
15	Deseret Inn	532-2900
16	Emerald Inn	533-9300
17	Salt Lake City Center TraveLodge	531-7100
		(800 255-3050)
18	Little America Hotel and Towers	363-6781 (800 453-9450)
19	Holiday Inn - Downtown	532-7000 (800 465-4329)
20	Quality Inn - City Center	521-2930 (800 221-2222 or 800 424-6423)
21	Embassy Suites Hotel	359-7800 (800 362-2779)
22	Super 8 Motel	534-0808 (800 843-1991)
23	Best Western Olympus Hotel	521-7373 (800 426-0722)

Map key courtesy the Salt Lake Convention & Visitors Bureau

MAP OF SALT LAKE CITY DOWNTOWN ACCOMMODATIONS

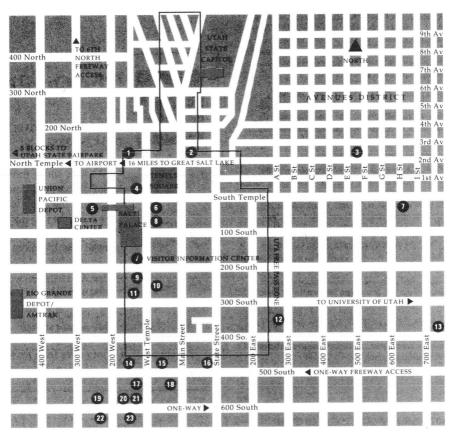

*UTAH TRANSIT AUTHORITY FREE FARE ZONE - RIDE FREE IF YOU ENTER AND EXIT THE BUS WITHIN THE BOUNDARIES OF THE FREE ZONE.

Map courtesy the Salt Lake Convention & Visitors Bureau

HISTORIC HOTEL UTAH

SALT LAKE CITY DOWNTOWN ATTRACTIONS

In Alphabetical Order

AMTRAK/Rio Grande Depot	33	364-8562
Beehive House	10	240-2671
Cathedral Church of St. Mark	25	322-3400
Catholic Cathedral of the Madeleine	26	328-8941
City and County Building	35	533-0858
Crossroads Plaza	15	531-1799
FAMILY HISTORY LIBRARY	**3**	**240-2331**
First Presbyterian Church	27	363-3889
Hansen Planetarium	12	538-2098
Hotel Utah	8	
LDS Church Office Building	6	240-3789
Lion House	9	363-5466
Museum of Church History and Art	4	240-3310
Salt Lake Art Center	2	328-4201
Salt Palace Convention Center	2	534-6370
Symphony Hall	2	533-5226
Temple Square	5	240-2534
Trolley Square	36	521-9877
Utah State Historical Society	33	533-5755
Utah State Capitol	21	538-3000
Visitor Information	1	521-2868
ZCMI Center Uptown	14	321-8745

(Key to downtown attractions map on the inside of back cover)

SALT LAKE CITY DOWNTOWN ATTRACTIONS

(Key to downtown attractions map on the inside of back cover)